D1642367

COUNTDOWN
BRITAIN'S STRATEGIC NUCLEAR FORCES

COUNTDOWN

BRITAIN'S STRATEGIC NUCLEAR FORCES

Air Vice-Marshal Stewart Menaul,
CB, CBE, DFC, AFC

ROBERT HALE · LONDON

First published in Great Britain 1980

ISBN 0 7091 8592 8

Robert Hale Limited
Clerkenwell House
Clerkenwell Green
London EC1R 0HT

Photoset by
Specialised Offset Services Limited, Liverpool
Printed in Great Britain by
Lowe & Brydone Ltd, Thetford, Norfolk
Bound by Weatherby Woolnough Ltd

CONTENTS

of Bomber Command — handover to the navy in 1968 without ceremony or thanks to the men and women who served in the independent nuclear deterrent — the end of Bomber Command, Britain no longer has an independent nuclear deterrent

LIST OF ILLUSTRATIONS

FOREWORD

Nuclear weapons have always been the subject of emotional controversy, more pronounced in this country than in any other. The United States, the most powerful nuclear nation on earth, has been testing nuclear weapons at the Nevada test site in the very heart of the American continent for more than thirty years without incident and with no interference or protest from minority groups of any kind, though they certainly have their fair share of them. Britain, on the other hand, has managed to maintain a nuclear capability since 1957, albeit a declining one, in the face of repeated attempts by a small minority of misguided people to compel successive Labour governments to rid the country of nuclear weapons and reduce the armed forces to some sort of vigilantes.

Unfortunately, during the past decade, Britain's nuclear power and the strength and capability of her armed forces have been eroded to a dangerously low level, which is only now being recognized as the result of serious discontent within the Forces the like of which has not been seen since the Invergordon mutiny.

A momentous decision awaits the Prime Minister and government of the day within months, rather than years. They must decide whether or not to replace the four Polaris submarines which today represent our only strategic nuclear force and which is assigned to the Supreme Allied Commander Europe as Britain's contribution to NATO nuclear forces. If they decide that it is in our interests to continue to contribute to this force, they must then decide what form the successor to Polaris should take.

The history of the British independent nuclear deterrent, which RAF Bomber Command maintained from 1957 to 1968, is littered

11

with examples of political chicanery, deliberate misrepresentation for ulterior political motives and inter-service rivalry and jealousy; the only redeeming feature being the loyalty and devotion to duty displayed by the men and women of the armed forces, particularly those of RAF Bomber Command. Never before in her long history has Britain possessed such a powerful military force, ready for action at less than four minutes warning night and day, year in and year out, for more than a decade. She will never again have an equivalent force.

The full story of Britain's strategic nuclear forces has not previously been told and it is important that those who make political decisions, no less than those who examine them critically, especially in the defence field, should know how such decisions were arrived at in the past and the effects they had on Britain's status as a power to influence events in Europe and on the world scene.

This short account of the strategic nuclear forces has been written mainly from personal experience and first-hand knowledge and is intended as a tribute to the men and women of all three Services who loyally carry out their duties despite scant recognition from their political masters, and all too often in the face of ill-informed criticism from a small but vocal minority who appear to owe allegiance to authorities beyond our shores.

Farnham   Stewart Menaul
Spring 1980

1

Nuclear Decision

Twenty-one years ago at the Pacific nuclear testing range based on Christmas Island in the Line Group, Britain demonstrated to the world that she had become a first rank independent nuclear power in her own right. In May 1957, the successful test of a thermonuclear weapon, or H-Bomb, dropped from a jet-engined Valiant bomber, brought to a close a series of tests with atomic and thermonuclear weapons that began with the testing of the first British nuclear device at the Monte Bello islands off the north-west coast of Australia in 1952. Both the weapons and the means of delivering them were entirely British, despite statements made by some politicians, aided and abetted by one or two national newspapers, who did their utmost at the time to discredit what must surely be acknowledged as one of this country's greatest achievements this century. Britain had become the third nuclear power in the world. It was the climax of a national effort in a highly technological arena, bristling with controversy from the moment the first nuclear weapon was tested at Alamogordo in New Mexico on 16th July 1945 — an event to which British scientists made a notable contribution.

The history of Britain's entry into the nuclear age has been brilliantly detailed by Margaret Gowing in "Independence and Deterrence: Britain and Atomic Energy 1945-52", published in 1974. The two volumes of this massive work chronicle the political decision-making processes that led to the formulation of a nuclear energy programme in 1946, the establishment of facilities for the production of fissile material and the atomic bomb. The period covered by Professor Gowing's book ends with the testing of the first nuclear device in 1952. The second element of a nuclear deterrent force, the means of delivery, was, if anything, more important and more difficult to produce than the atom bomb, and there were many obstacles to be surmounted in the process.

In the period after the war, conditions could hardly have been less conducive to the design, production and procurement of new aircraft, which were the only known means of delivery at that time against targets in the only country likely to pose a threat to Britain's security for as far ahead as could be foreseen – the Soviet Union. That Britain had the expertise within her world-renowned aircraft industry to manufacture suitable aircraft there was no doubt. She also had considerable knowledge and experience in the nuclear field in peace and war, which was not generally appreciated, though generous tribute had been paid by the United States to the part played by British scientists in solving the mystery of the structure of matter, the secret of the atom and how its energy could be released in explosive form.

Britain's interest in, and contribution to, the scientific exploration of the mystery of matter, the structure of the atom and nuclear energy goes back a long way, to the beginning of the nineteenth century, when a chemist named Dalton propounded a theory on the structure of matter that improved on the ideas of the Greek philosopher Democritus more than four hundred years before Christ. Dalton, in experiments to study how elements combined to form compounds, concluded that elements were composed of small indestructible particles of matter called atoms, that all atoms of the same element were alike, and atoms of one element differed from those of another simply by weight.

Nearly a century later scientists in Europe, particularly British scientists, not satisfied with Dalton's explanations of the structure of matter, were probing deeper, and eventually their combined efforts led Niels Bohr, a Danish physicist, to suggest that atoms were not solid particles, but resembled small solar systems, with a central nucleus round which smaller particles circulated. J.J. Thomson found that the particles circulating around the central nucleus were negatively charged, and he called them electrons. The two main particles, making up the central nucleus, were also discovered by British scientists. Ernest Rutherford determined the fundamental particle of which all matter is composed, the positively charged nucleus of the hydrogen atom, which he called the proton, and, to complete the trinity, James Chadwick detected the uncharged particle in the nucleus, which he called the neutron.

In the 1930s, the university town of Gottingen in Germany was the Mecca for nuclear physicists from all over the world. Science knows no frontiers of race, colour or creed; Hitler had not yet begun his persecution of the Jews, or his rampage over Europe, so great names like Einstein, Oppenheimer, Weizacker, Frisch, Meitner and Hahn met to discuss the developing and fascinating subject of nuclear energy. But as the political climate in Germany deteriorated, and Hitler launched his attack on the Jews, international collaboration in nuclear physics came to a halt. Einstein, Oppenheimer and others escaped to America; others, again, went to Sweden, and a few, including Frisch, made their way to Britain. Many of Germany's best scientists, of course, remained in Germany to continue their work in the nuclear field and to pose the horrifying possibility that if they succeeded in creating a nuclear explosion by fissioning the atoms of uranium, Hitler would acquire the atom bomb to add to the mighty war machine which he had created by 1939, when World War II began.

United States physicists were so alarmed by the prospect that they persuaded Einstein to write to President Roosevelt, drawing attention to the work on which they were all engaged and the catastrophic consequences for the rest of Europe and the world, if Germany should solve the problem of fission reaction before any other country. In Britain, in 1940, Frisch and Peierls were advising Ministers and the Chiefs of Staff of the possibility of creating nuclear explosions by fission of uranium and, as a result, the Maud Committee was set up to examine various proposals and report on their feasibility. But the Japanese attack on Pearl Harbour in 1941 brought the United States into the war, and Churchill and Roosevelt agreed to pool resources in nuclear research in an attempt to establish a practical method of creating a fission explosion. The great Manhattan Project was launched to direct and co-ordinate all scientific and industrial effort devoted to nuclear research and among its many distinguished physicists, including some who had recently escaped from Germany, were a number from Britain, led by W.G. Penney, later to become the driving force in Britain's nuclear weapons programme. The British contingent made a valuable contribution to the success of the Manhattan Project and were present at the testing of the world's first atomic explosion, code-named Operation Trinity, at Alamogordo in New Mexico on 16th July 1945.

The success of Operation Trinity was conveyed to President Truman (who had become President of the United States on the death of Roosevelt), at Potsdam, where the heads of the Allied nations were meeting to discuss European problems. Truman informed Stalin of this momentous achievement, but the Marshal apparently showed neither interest nor emotion. Attlee had replaced Churchill as Prime Minister, following the Labour victory in the General Election of 1945, and knew nothing of the Manhattan Project until briefed by the defence staff when he became Prime Minister. The war against Japan was still being waged with mounting intensity by the United States, Britain and the Commonwealth, and fierce fighting was in prospect as Japan was slowly but remorselessly driven back from the territories she had occupied in four years of conquest. That she would defend her island kingdom to the bitter end there was no doubt and in the process inflict heavy casualties on United States and allied armies.

The decision to use the atomic bomb against Japan was taken by President Truman on the advice of a committee of distinguished scientists and military leaders, and on 6th August 1945, a B-29 bomber, nicknamed *Enola Gay*, dropped the first bomb on Hiroshima with devastating effect. A similar attack a few days later on the city of Nagasaki brought about the surrender of Japan, the end of the war, and a storm of protest from moralists and pacifists on both sides of the Atlantic, to which some of the scientists who had so recently worked on the Manhattan Project lent their support. Despite the euphoria which a return to peace generated (there was a genuine feeling that this time the war to end all war had been concluded) agitation against atomic weapons was smouldering in the United States and in Britain. The Labour Government, elected in 1945, had among its members an assortment of Communist fellow-travellers, conscientious objectors and pacifists whom Ernest Bevin, the Foreign Secretary, distrusted implicitly, though Attlee tolerated them. But even Attlee is on record as saying to Professor John MacIntosh in an interview that he thought some of his Cabinet colleagues were not fit to be trusted with secret or sensitive information. Small wonder that the decision that Britain should become a nuclear power was taken in secrecy by a small select committee without the approval of Parliament or, indeed, consultation with the full Cabinet.

The political environment in Europe and throughout the world in the period 1946 to 1949, during which Britain decided on a nuclear programme, the manufacture of atomic bombs and the means of delivering them, had a profound effect on debates in political and military circles, not only on nuclear affairs but on the whole concept of future grand strategy, weapons systems, and the defence of Britain and the Commonwealth. Immediately after the surrender of Japan, the Soviet Union was the only potential enemy likely to pose a threat to Europe for at least a decade. The ruthlessness and brutality with which they began to assert their hegemony over eastern Europe surprised even those who had warned of their political aspirations in the post-war period.

At the time of the German surrender in 1945, total allied forces in Europe numbered about $4\frac{1}{2}$ million men, of which the United States contributed some three million. Only one year later the figure had fallen to less than a million, as British and American forces were rapidly demobilized. The liberated countries, France, Belgium, Netherlands, Norway and Denmark, had virtually no armed forces and were slowly recovering from four years of occupation by a harsh and demanding regime. The Soviet Union, meanwhile, had maintained armed forces numbering nearly four million on a full war footing, most of them in Eastern Europe. The Paris Peace Conference of 1946 drew up peace treaties with Italy, Finland, Bulgaria, Hungary and Roumania, which were signed in 1947, but similar meetings in Moscow and London failed to agree on the future of Germany and Austria, mainly because of Russian intransigence.

The wartime annexation by the Soviet Union of Estonia, Latvia and Lithuania, together with the occupation of Poland, Czechoslovakia, Hungary and the eastern half of Germany, coupled with infiltration and subversion of the governments of Albania, Bulgaria and Roumania, completed the territorial expansion of the Soviet Union in Eastern Europe, leaving the way clear for political pressure on

17

Western Europe. The Kremlin tried unsuccessfully to intimidate Turkey, to gain bases along the Dardanelles; and in Greece a guerrilla campaign which began in 1944, became a full scale war by 1946. In northern Iran the Soviets attempted to obtain a foothold as a stepping-stone to their long dreamed of expansion southwards to the Gulf and the Indian Ocean. The signing of the United Nations Charter in San Francisco in June 1945, made little impression on the Soviet Union, despite the euphoria surrounding what it was hoped would be the world peace organization to outlaw war on this planet. There were many statesmen in the West, however, who doubted man's willingness or ability to transform human nature to the extent that international disputes could or would in future be settled by peaceful means round the conference table.

The Soviet Union had already begun to consolidate the territorial gains which had accrued to her in the bitter journey of reconquest from the very gates of Moscow to Berlin and beyond in World War II. The Kremlin had indicated that 'liberated' countries of Eastern Europe would remain under Soviet control until peace treaties with Germany and Austria were concluded and frontiers settled. To emphasize the point, signs of more permanent occupation were becoming evident. The Western powers had totally failed to under-stand the mentality of the Russian leaders or their evolving strategy, despite Churchill's warnings, even before the war, when he described Russia as "a riddle, wrapped in a mystery inside an enigma".

By 1947, despite the wartime alliance, Soviet intentions were becoming clear. They were bent on securing a new, centralized German government within a communist satellite system, directed from Moscow as part of a more ambitious world plan to promote the doctrines of Marx and Lenin. An "iron curtain" descended across Europe, and in 1948 the Berlin blockade was an unmistakable indicator of future Soviet policy. It was also a test of Western will and unity. Fortunately this blatant attempt at intimidation was resisted, and the blockade which lasted almost a year was defeated in 1949, mainly by the success of a massive airlift which kept the inhabitants of Berlin alive. When the blockade was finally lifted, Berlin had become a divided city. The Soviet sector was effectively isolated politically from the Western zones, but physical movement between east and west was still possible. Throughout the 1950s relations between the two power blocs became increasingly strained, until in 1961 the infamous Berlin Wall totally separated east from west, except for one or two strictly controlled check points. The Russians had achieved their objective of converting East Germany into the so-called German Democratic Republic within the Soviet satellite system, but they had failed to create a unified Germany under Communist control.

In these immediate post-war years, Western European countries, sensitive to the dangers that still confronted them, were seeking to fashion alliances within the framework of the United Nations Charter. In 1947, Britain and France signed the Dunkirk Treaty of mutual assistance, while other countries were contemplating similar treaties aimed at eliminating future conflict in Europe in the event of a resurgent Germany. But the 1948 *coup d'état* in Prague, which put Czechoslovakia firmly into the Soviet camp, added a note of urgency to the deliberations taking place on the future structure of European defence, and identified the real potential enemy. In 1948, Britain, France, Belgium, Luxembourg and the Netherlands signed the Brussels Treaty, to deter armed aggression in Europe and provide mutual assistance in the event of armed attack.

While European countries were concerning themselves with matters affecting their security, the United States Senate had begun to consider that of the whole North Atlantic region. Canada proposed the formation of a wider organization, which the United States and Britain welcomed. It was to supersede the Brussels Treaty and include more members. In April 1949, negotiations having been completed, and despite Soviet denunciation and veiled threats, the North Atlantic Treaty Organization (NATO) was signed in Washington. There were twelve signatories to the treaty, which consisted of a preamble and fourteen articles, including Article 5 providing specifically for collective defence in the event of attack on any member from whatever source.

During the difficult period between 1945 and 1947, when Europe was trying to recover from the ravages of war and had become thoroughly alarmed by the attitudes and activities of the Communists in Eastern Europe, France and Italy, the United States President in a speech to Congress declared that, "It must be the policy of the United

States of America to support free peoples who are resisting attempted subjugation by armed minorities or by outside pressure". This became known as the Truman doctrine, and was implemented immediately in the form of aid to Greece and Turkey against which Soviet pressure had been most severe. In June 1947, the United States Secretary of State, General George C. Marshall launched a massive programme of economic assistance to European countries who needed it. The Marshall Plan was instrumental in ensuring the economic recovery of friendly nations and called at least a temporary halt to Communist propaganda and subversive activity in Western Europe. But in 1948 in the Far East, the Malayan emergency began and the ensuing struggle against Communist insurgency was to last for twelve years. It was only one of the so-called wars of liberation, supported by China and the Soviet Union, that have kept the world in a state of tension, sometimes bordering on chaos, since the end of World War II.

It was against this background, in an atmosphere of uncertainty at home and menacing problems abroad, that the British Government had to decide whether to become a military nuclear power and attempt to retain some semblance of the political power and influence which Britain had wielded in pre-war years when circumstances were very different from those prevailing in 1946, or to bow to the economic realities of the post-war situation and accept a status somewhat less than that of a Great Power.

When the 1947 Cabinet papers were released to the Public Record Office in January 1978, under the thirty-year rule, the minutes of the committee which took the historic decision that Britain should produce atomic bombs were not among them. This committee, known as GEN 163, was chaired by Prime Minister Clement Attlee and among its members were Bevin, Morrison, Alexander, Addison and Wilmot. All that has been made known about the deliberations of the committee is that the first item on the agenda for discussion was "Research in atomic weapons". The minutes of this committee meeting will not be released until 1998, but it is known that certain proposals made by Lord Portal, who had been appointed Controller of Production (Atomic Energy), were approved by the committee. Portal, as wartime Chief of the Air Staff, had access to all reports and papers of the highest security classification pertaining to the wartime

Manhattan Project, the development and testing of the first atomic bomb and the effects of such weapons when used against towns or industrial complexes in war. He was better informed than anyone else in Britain on the likely effects of the new weapons on future defence strategy and particularly air strategy.

When appointed to his new post, Portal took special care to safeguard the secrets which Britain had acquired by virtue of the presence of British scientists and Air Force officers at the laboratories, test ranges and other organizations in the United States during the period of the Manhattan Project and on an operational flight when an atomic bomb was dropped on a Japanese city. Portal shared Attlee's opinion on the reliability and loyalty of some of the members of the Cabinet, and it was he who suggested that the proceedings of the GEN 163 Committee should have a fifty-year embargo imposed. The Secretary of the Committee, D.H.F. Rickett, duly applied this restriction when the minutes were sent to archives. In retrospect, to anyone who has been involved in nuclear affairs in the post-war era, the manner in which decisions were taken by GEN 163 was entirely correct and appropriate. Some members of the Labour Government greatly admired the Soviet Union and its leader, Stalin, but they appeared to be incapable of seeing further than the wartime alliance. Some of them even advocated a new alliance with the Soviet Union in preference to a similar association with the United States. Fortunately, the government had Ernest Bevin as Foreign Secretary and such ideas were not entertained. Bevin and his military advisers recognized what Churchill had been saying for years, that the threat to Europe would come from the Soviet Union and it was imperative that the United States should be closely associated with arrangements for security and defence. It was perhaps just a coincidence that the NATO alliance was formed in 1949, the same year that the Soviet Union tested their first nuclear weapon.

When Britain finally embarked on her nuclear programme, she did so without the direct assistance that many people had come to expect from the United States. Nevertheless, the programme was launched despite some opposition, but without any real knowledge of how long it would take to produce operational atomic weapons and the means of delivering them. It is sometimes suggested that the decision to become a nuclear power was motivated solely by a misplaced concept of authority and influence, and that atomic weapons were seen simply as a symbol of independence and great power status. But Ernest Bevin is on record as saying, "We could not afford to acquiesce in an American monopoly of this new development". He might have added that it was only a matter of time before the Soviet Union joined the nuclear club. Those who have been intimately connected with Britain's nuclear programme and the creation of the independent nuclear deterrent, know that militarily the decisions were based on sound strategic appreciations, coinciding closely with United States Air Force (USAF) thinking in the post-war years. Politically, there may have been mistaken ideas on Britain's future role in world affairs, which influenced the decision to become a nuclear power, but militarily the issue was never in doubt, at least so far as the Air Force was concerned.

Some government scientific advisers like Professor P.M. Blackett, opposed Britain's nuclear programme, but his views carried little weight except among his own kind. Professor Lindemann (later Viscount Cherwell), who was Churchill's principal scientific adviser, had no doubts and fully supported the programme right up to the final test phases in Australia and at Christmas Island.

During the critical years when plants for the production of plutonium 239 and uranium 235, the essential fissile materials for nuclear weapons, were being constructed, and an Atomic Energy Research Establishment was being formed at Harwell, intense debate was taking place in the Air Ministry and at the Staff Colleges and other military academic institutions, on the impact of atomic weapons on future strategy and the future of air power. In June 1945, a committee of scientists, under the chairmanship of Sir Henry Tizard, completed a study for the Chiefs of Staff on impending developments in warfare, based on the rapid technological progress that had taken place in conventional weapons design and the means of delivering them, in the closing stages of the war. Radar, electronics, the jet engine and the ballistic rocket were but four of the inventions that were bound to have a profound effect on future weapons and the tactics adopted for their application. The committee concluded, *inter alia*, that Britain could not forgo the atomic bomb, even if the only

22

use for it, as perceived in 1945, was in retaliation for attack on this country.

Inter-Service rivalry and jealousy, which many senior officers in all three Services hoped had been eliminated during the war years, became prevalent again when discussions on future strategy, doctrine and weapons systems were undertaken in the immediate post-war years, especially when the atomic bomb was presented as a new and revolutionary weapon. The Army and Navy were determined to protect their interests against what they saw as the threat from the RAF. One rear-admiral described the atomic bomb in somewhat scathing terms as "just a bigger and better bomb", and in the light of the knowledge available outside a select circle, privy to all the information on the atomic bomb and its effects, such an attitude was perhaps understandable. To the RAF, which had made such a massive contribution to victory in World War II, not only by the strategic bombing campaign against Germany and Italy, but in accounting for a greater tonnage of enemy ships and submarines than the Navy, the atomic bomb was the weapon that would justify the continuation of a strategic bombing force as the primary instrument of deterrence and the major delivery system for conventional or nuclear weapons in any future war. There were no delivery vehicles other than manned bombers available in 1947, or likely to become available in the decade ahead; and there was no country in Europe except Britain capable of undertaking the creation of a nuclear bomber force.

It is not true to say, as Professor Gowing does, that in 1947 the RAF were designing aircraft in ignorance of the size and character of the weapons they might have to carry. Not only did RAF officers fly on one of the missions against Japanese cities in which an atomic bomb was dropped, but liaison between RAF Bomber Command and the United States Air Force, established during the war when the US 8th Air Force operated alongside Bomber Command in the successful strategic offensive against Germany, was maintained post-war. Those responsible for operational requirements for new bomber aircraft knew the size of American atomic bombs and the precise measurements of the bomb-bay of a B-29. When specifications for three new jet bombers were drawn up, the RAF knew exactly what they wanted and why they wanted it. The doctrine for the employment

23

of nuclear weapons in 1946 was relatively simple and vastly different from the complex requirements for nuclear deterrence and nuclear war-fighting capability needed today.

In 1952, the efforts of the scientific and industrial organizations engaged on the production of fissile material and the design of nuclear weapons had produced enough plutonium for the assembly of a nuclear device ready for testing. With the agreement of the Australian Government, a suitable test site was established at the Monte Bello islands off the north-west coast of Australia. An old Royal Navy frigate, HMS *Plym*, with the atomic device on board was anchored in a lagoon among the islands and suitably instrumented. When all the necessary safety precautions had been taken, the device was exploded; *Plym* was vaporized and the test declared successful. It had taken more than six years from the initial decision to produce fissile material suitable for an atomic device to the completion of a successful test, but in retrospect, bearing in mind the manifold difficulties confronting our scientists and industrialists in the harsh economic climate of the post-war years, it was a creditable performance. Unfortunately, the Russians succeeded in testing their first nuclear bomb in 1949, confounding experts on both sides of the Atlantic, who thought they could not produce an atomic bomb for testing until 1952 at the earliest. In 1953, Britain tested another nuclear device at a test site called Emu Field, near Woomera, in central Australia. This was also successful within the parameters set, but it was to be three more years before the first atomic bomb suitable for carriage by a bomber was successfully tested.

The first atomic bombs produced by Britain were based on what was called the implosion system, using a fissile core of plutonium 239. There were at that time two methods of creating an atomic explosion, using either plutonium 239 or uranium 235, both of which had been tested by the United States. One was known as the gun principle, in which two sub-critical, semi-spherical masses of fissile material were kept apart in a device resembling a gun barrel. A suitable mechanism was installed to fire an explosive charge, which literally shot the two half spheres together with great force, thereby causing the fissile mass to become critical. At the instant of contact, a neutron source was introduced, which began the fission process in a chain reaction. As each atom of the fissile material absorbed a neutron and fissioned, three neutrons were simultaneously produced to fission more atoms of the fissile material. The whole process took place in millionths of a second and the resultant release of energy was a violent explosion. Some of the multiplying neutrons, of course, tended to escape, so a shielding substance, or tamper, was used to deflect stray neutrons back into the core and thereby improve efficiency.

The gun method was not very effective, so a different technique was employed in which the sub-critical plutonium fissile core was machined in the form of a hollow sphere, at the centre of which was a neutron source. The core was surrounded by a carefully machined sphere of high explosive, armed with a firing mechanism that would produce a near-perfect, convergent, spherical pressure wave, acting equally and simultaneously on the surface of the spherical fissile core, thus compressing, or imploding, it into a critical mass. The process of fission and a chain reaction took place as before and stray neutrons were deflected by the use of a heavy material surrounding the whole mechanism. Over the years, many improvements have been made in the design of nuclear weapons, giving better performance, greater yield-to-weight ratio, improved 'burning' efficiency of the fissile material and variable yields in the explosive power of the weapon which can be selected by the user. The descriptions outlined above are, of course, very much over-simplified. In the early days of nuclear weapons the physical size of the atomic bomb for a given yield was much greater than it is today, mainly because the techniques of arming, fusing and firing a weapon which had to be carried in an aircraft were not then as refined.

Having mastered the technique of fission, in which the atoms of a suitable heavy element are split apart to release energy in a violent form, scientists had at their disposal an essential requirement to achieve the opposite process of fusing atoms of light elements together, to form other, heavier elements. In the process, energy would be released in a violent explosion. The fusion materials commonly used are the isotopes of hydrogen (the lightest element) called deuterium and tritium. But in order to fuse particles of these elements together, it is necessary to make them collide with extreme force. One method of doing this is to heat the material to a very high temperature, of the order of millions of degrees centigrade. There is as yet no known method of achieving this satisfactorily except by atomic reaction. If, therefore, deuterium and tritium nuclei are introduced into a fission assembly, the temperatures which occur in the fission reaction are sufficient to fuse the light nuclei together, with a resultant release of energy in explosive form. There is no limit to the yield of weapon that might be produced by this process, it depends in the main on the amount of fusion material used, but the yield of such weapons is measured in megatons (millions of tons) as compared with kilotons (thousands of tons) for atomic weapons. A further process, known as secondary fission, or fission-fusion-fission, became possible when the fusion process had been mastered. Natural uranium 238 does not fission in the normal fission reaction which is achieved with relatively slow neutrons. But it will fission with fast neutrons. Since uranium 238 is a good material for a tamper to prevent the escape of neutrons, and the neutrons generated in a fusion reaction are very fast, it is possible to fission the uranium 238 in a fusion reaction.

While British scientists were designing and testing atomic bombs in the early 1950s, they were also solving the problems associated with thermonuclear, or hydrogen, weapons based on the fusion principle. When they designed and produced operational atomic weapons suitable for carriage on V-bombers, the first of which was tested in October 1956, they had also produced thermonuclear weapons which were tested in 1957.

2

Nuclear Strategy

While the politicians with their scientific and military advisers were closeted in their *ad hoc* secret committees, establishing the research, development and production facilities for the manufacture of atomic bombs, the Air Ministry was deeply involved in the equally, if not more, important task of drawing up operational requirements for new aircraft. These bombers had to be capable of operating in a strategic role with either nuclear or conventional weapons at ranges exceeding considerably those which Bomber Command had been accustomed to in World War II. The manned bomber was the only means of delivering conventional or nuclear weapons over long distances at the end of World War II, despite the introduction by Germany of the first effective ballistic rockets in the closing stages of the war. There was abundant evidence of the practicability and effectiveness of the combination of the long-range bomber and the atomic bomb from the United States Army Air Force attacks on Japan, and it was known that Dr Oppenheimer and his brilliant team of scientists in the United States had embarked on the creation of a variation on the atomic theme, involving a process of fusion of atomic particles, as opposed to fission; but the effects of such a weapon were at that time unknown.

In Britain, in 1946, it was generally accepted in scientific and military circles that the two atomic bombs dropped on Japan, though different in design, produced the same effects, and that all atomic bombs would behave in a similar manner. The idea of selective yields for attacking different types of targets did not enter into discussions on military tactics, and only a relatively few individuals appreciated the significance of fission weapons based on plutonium 239 as the fissile core and those which used the alternative material, uranium

27

235. The strategy of nuclear deterrence was born when the atomic bomb was dropped on Hiroshima, even though it was not universally acknowledged, and was to be the dominant concept in strategic planning over many years. It was the genuine belief of some politicians and military men that the effects of the weapon were so appalling, particularly the blast and radiation effects, that no one would dare to use them. They would act as a deterrent to any would-be aggressor and would never again be used in anger.

In Air Force circles, discussions were more realistic and centred around the catastrophic damage that the atomic bomb could inflict on targets such as towns and industrial complexes, and how the effects of such weapons might be applied to land and sea warfare as well as in strategic air war. It is a popular fallacy among present-day amateur academic strategists that the advent of the atomic bomb in 1945 was so shattering, that serious debate in military circles on the future conduct of war was paralysed; that the Clausewitzian description of war as a continuation of policy by other means was obsolete and demanded urgent reappraisal. Some even make the ludicrous suggestion that it was not until the 1960s, when United States academics began to take an interest in military strategy, that intelligent debate on nuclear weapons became apparent. Nothing could be further from the truth. When the United States Air Force, continuing the practice first established in Britain of involving scientists in military planning, invited the Rand Corporation to undertake certain studies on their behalf, they were encouraging a wider debate on future war, the development of weapons systems, and the strategy and tactics for their employment. This principle now has widespread application and, although many excellent ideas have been forthcoming from academic institutes on a whole range of subjects in the military field, it is pertinent to point out that many others had already been thought of by military planners and either rejected or acted upon before they were suggested from outside sources. Papers on war strategy and weapons systems, prepared in the Ministry of Defence, Staff Colleges, or other Service organizations, are usually graded 'Top Secret', and thereby not available to the general public, so academic strategists were not aware of the discussions taking place.

The introduction of the atomic bomb certainly demanded a

reappraisal of the Principles of War as expounded by Clausewitz and taught with almost religious fervour in Staff Colleges throughout Europe in pre-war days. Concentration of force, for example, took on a new meaning in the light of the effects of nuclear weapons, when it was realized that a single bomber carrying a single atomic bomb could achieve the same result against an enemy city, town or industrial complex, as had required hundreds of bombers armed with conventional high explosive bombs in World War II. What was even more significant was the fact that it could achieve its objective in a few minutes.

There was, of course, divided opinion among military men on concepts of strategy for future wars. It was thought by some military strategists that the days of the classical land and sea battles were over, including those of the type conducted in Europe, the Middle East, and Far East in World War II; whole armies and navies could now be wiped out in a few minutes and this meant that the overwhelming influence of British sea power, for example, was gone forever – it was gone, anyway, but for different reasons which military strategists had not yet recognized. Another view, widely held in 1945 even before the decision by Attlee and his committee that Britain should become a nuclear power, was that the deterrent effect of the atomic bomb would be so great as to *outlaw war itself* as we had known it – a view shared by Portal when still Chief of the Air Staff. Not all military opinion agreed with Portal, of course, and there is no denying that the Army and Navy at that time were more concerned with their future than with intellectual discussion on strategic studies in the nuclear age. They were fearful lest the Air Force should become the primary instrument of Britain's future defence capability, just as the Army was after World War I and throughout the 1930s, even to the extent of frustrating proposals for the proper use of air power in modern war, which contributed to Britain's unpreparedness for World War II.

It is important to recall that in 1945 only the United States had nuclear weapons and the means of delivering them. Some politicians and military strategists advocated that all future bombing should be left to the Americans. The more perceptive members of the Labour Government realized that it was only a question of time before other industrialized countries would seek to acquire them – including the Soviet Union. It was appreciated, therefore, that future British strategy would have to take account of the fact that other countries, friends as well as potential enemies, could become nuclear powers, and that future doctrine and strategy would have to cater for the possibility that Britain, whose Empire and Commonwealth had not yet disintegrated, might have to conduct limited conventional wars in which air power would play a dominant role, as it had done in pre-war days, despite opposition from the Army. In formulating doctrine and strategy in the post-war period, the RAF took careful cognizance of the service strategies of pre-war years, such as they were.

British strategy in the 1930s and throughout the war is still a contentious subject, on which serious students of military strategy have often expressed diametrically opposed views. The concept of Grand Strategy, dating from the time of Napoleon and accepted by most European countries, emphasized the importance of mobilizing the entire resources of a nation or nations – economic, financial, industrial and material, as well as armed forces – in order to confront the enemy with superior forces. In formulating Grand Strategy, government ministers, senior officers of the armed forces and advisers from outside government departments were usually involved. Below the level of Grand Strategy, there was Maritime Strategy, Combined Strategy, Air Strategy, etc, and unless the level at which strategy was being thought of was defined, the result was liable to be confusing.

Prior to 1939, British strategy and that of her European allies at all levels was totally unrealistic, and failed to prepare the Alliance for the inevitable clash with Germany. After the fall of France and the Low Countries in 1940, Britain, the Commonwealth and, later, the United States, adopted strategies on an *ad hoc* basis, making do with the resources that became available and the armed forces that could be conscripted, trained and equipped as conditions allowed. For two years after the débâcle on the European continent, the defeat of Britain's armies and the humiliation of Dunkirk, the only force capable of direct offensive action against the enemy in his homeland was RAF Bomber Command, which operated continuously from September 1939 until May 1945 when Germany was defeated. In other words, offensive Air Strategy was the only strategy that Britain could adopt in those dangerous and depressing years.

In 1943, the Air Ministry issued a comprehensive twelve-part paper on the "Role of the RAF in War and the Strategical use of Air Power". This excellent paper, designed for use in Staff Colleges and other service academic training establishments, had been updated to include some of the lessons learned in the first two years of war. Part Six, devoted to a study of strategy, included Policy, Grand Strategy, Service Strategy and its triangular forms. It described strategy as essentially a process of purposeful reasoning, governing the manipulation of warlike resources and armed forces. The reader was advised not to "go away with the idea that because we have talked of strategy mostly in connection with high councillors of State and Service Chiefs that it is an exotic cult. It is sheer common sense applied to war". That sums up Clausewitz in a nutshell. His real claim to immortality is not so much what he said, since most of it was common sense applied to military affairs, but the fact that he took the trouble to write it down, not only for the benefit of his Royal pupil, Crown Prince Frederick William of Prussia, but for future generations of aspiring military strategists.

Dealing specifically with Air Strategy, the Air Ministry paper placed great stress on the importance of the offensive which was exemplified by Bomber Command during the war, particularly in the last $2\frac{1}{2}$ years, when they had the tools necessary for the job. Throughout the war, therefore, the RAF paid particular attention to the role of air power, the need for changes in strategy and tactics from time to time, and the important principles to be observed in the exercise of air power. In 1947, Marshal of the Royal Air Force Lord Tedder, perhaps the greatest Chief of the Air Staff since Trenchard, delivered the Lees Knowles lectures at Cambridge, in which he dealt with the unities of war, the indivisibility of air power, air superiority and the exercise of air power. He pointed out that at the peak of the war, bomber operations took approximately 12 per cent of the direct war effort and averaged over the whole war only 7 per cent. In addition to the devastating effects the bomber offensive had on Germany's war making capacity, contributing more than any other single factor to their inability to continue the war, Tedder emphasized that the battle for air superiority over Europe, prior to the landing of allied forces on the Normandy beaches, was achieved not by fighters, but by bombers. It was in the night skies over Germany that the crucial battle for air superiority was decided. The Battle of Germany was a more intense struggle than the Battle of Britain, and it lasted six years as opposed to sixteen weeks, and cost the lives of 55,000 aircrew as opposed to 650 in the Battle of Britain. As von Rundstedt put it, it was "all a question of air force, air force and again air force". Summing up his own views on air power in war, Tedder said, "I am utterly convinced that the outstanding and vital lesson of this last war is that air power is the dominant factor in this modern world and that, though the methods of exercising it will change, it will remain the dominant factor so long as power determines the fate of nations." Field Marshal Montgomery agreed with him.

The RAF were under no illusions about the importance of air power for the future defence of these islands and the role which strategic offensive air power would be likely to play in both nuclear and conventional operations. In 1946, the Chief of the Air Staff submitted to the Ministry of Supply a formal requirement for the atomic bomb, followed a few weeks later by an operational requirement for new strategic bombers. The Minister of Defence, A.V. Alexander, a man of no great standing in the Labour Government and with little knowledge of military affairs, raised no objections to either request, nor were they the subject of parliamentary or public debate. But even in those early days of the development of the British nuclear deterrent, there were pro-Communist elements both in the government and the country who wished to see Britain disarmed, despite warnings by the government itself, as well as by Churchill and others, that a ruthless military power occupied half of Europe and posed a serious threat to the other half; that its aims were to impose its ideology on the rest of mankind, by force if necessary. This disreputable minority was to expand its activities in the years ahead, and eventually became the Campaign for Nuclear Disarmament (CND), led by woolly-minded left-wing Labour politicians, parsons and renegade students with nothing better to occupy their time.

The agitation against nuclear weapons and against the British nuclear deterrent over the years achieved nothing, except to earn the contempt of the armed forces and provide an irritant to the vast majority of sensible people throughout the country. CND supporters were, however, exploitable and Harold Wilson, leader of the Labour Party made full political capital out of their activities in the run-up to the 1964 General Election.

By 1947, Britain had embarked on a programme to produce nuclear weapons and the bombers for delivering them. At the same time, Minister of Defence, Alexander, announced the introduction of the Ten Year Rule, directing that in planning military strategy and weapon requirements for the future it should be assumed that there would be no major war for at least ten years. A similar procedure, equally ill-conceived with dire consequences for our defences in the years that followed, was introduced after World War I. In neither case did the procedure have the support of the Chiefs of Staff; it was a purely political decision that was to be an obstacle to realistic planning and economic and speedy production of the elements of an effective independent nuclear deterrent.

In the economic climate prevailing post-war, no one knew how long it would take to produce either the atom bomb or the bombers for delivering them, and even inspired guesses were of little help. There was a massive collection of wartime aircraft and equipment which the government were determined should be used for as long as possible. The RAF, like the other Services, had undergone a rapid, almost indecent, run-down at the end of the war, and the 1946 Defence White Paper emphasized that extensive research and development into new weapons systems would take priority over further production of current systems, even with improvements in performance already specified. The RAF ended the war with more than 2,500 Lancaster, Halifax and Mosquito bombers which had given superb service in attacks on German and Italian targets. The radar, navigation and bombing equipment fitted to some of these aircraft (not all) in the latter years of the war enabled crews to find and bomb targets in all weathers, by day or night. But the range of all three types was limited and unless they operated from forward bases in Europe they could not reach targets in the Soviet Union. A successor to the Lancaster was under production at the end of the war, planned for operations in the Far East and the Pacific, but its range was little better than that of the Lancaster and its performance in other respects was such that it too

33

was unsuitable for operations against the Soviet Union. Nevertheless, the RAF had accepted the Lincoln, as it became known, and, as events turned out, Bomber Command had to operate it for eight years from 1946. It was grossly inferior to the United States B-29, which had entered service with the USAAF units in the Pacific in 1944 and had demonstrated its ability to operate in the conventional or nuclear role over long ranges. The United States was already developing jet-engined bombers, made possible by Britain's transfer of jet engine technology before the war ended, and it was also known that American scientists and engineers were exploring the possibility of further development of the ballistic rocket, the German V2, of which they had captured examples in the closing months of the war, together with its inventor, Wernher von Braun.

3

The V-Bombers

Towards the end of the war a new and revolutionary system of propulsion for aircraft was introduced into operational service by Britain and Germany. It had been evolved from a British invention which took shape more than sixteen years earlier in experiments conducted by a cadet at the Royal Air Force College, Cranwell, and reached a climax on 15th May 1941, when the Gloster E-28/39 flew for the first time with a Whittle jet engine as its motive power. The inventor was Air Commodore Sir Frank Whittle, and his jet engine principle eventually provided the basic power units around which the massive nuclear bomber forces of the United States, Britain and Russia were built in the 1950s.

The E-28/39 was a small, clean, streamlined aircraft with a single engine mounted in the fuselage. It had a tricycle undercarriage and short, stubby wings. The absence of a propeller was immediately apparent to the onlooker and gave the aircraft a somewhat naked and uncanny appearance. The engine developed about 1,600 pounds of thrust, permitting speeds of over 400 mph to be attained, but range and endurance were both very restricted. Nevertheless, the aircraft demonstrated the potential of jet propulsion for future military and civil aircraft and fully vindicated Whittle's faith in his invention.

The Germans and Italians also carried out research on jet engines, but by the end of the war there were only a few jet fighters in service in Europe and only one (German) bomber. The brief appearance of Germany's products in the dying months of the war created something of a sensation, and demonstrated that Germany, despite her pre-occupation with impending defeat, had managed to produce an extremely good interceptor jet fighter. But, of course, her need was greater than ours; it was, in fact, desperate, due to the unrelenting attentions of Bomber Command and the United States 8th Air Force, pounding German cities and industrial complexes in a round-the-clock offensive unparalleled in the history of air warfare.

Among the many honours conferred on Sir Frank Whittle, perhaps the most significant took place in December 1964 when he was named as the first recipient of the Goddard Award of the American Institute of Aeronautics and Astronautics. The citation stated that the award had been made for, "Imagination, skill, persistence and courage in pioneering the gas turbine as a jet propulsion aircraft engine, thus revolutionizing military and commercial aviation for all time. His contribution was primarily an engineering one, but his skill in synthesizing the talents of others into solving the tremendous technical problems needed to turn an idea into a practical lightweight engine makes him the father of the jet age; his jet engine reached America before the end of the war to lay the foundation of the entire post-war American aircraft industry". This tribute is similar to that paid to Rutherford, who was acknowledged as "the father of nuclear physics". But it was not only to the Americans that Britain transferred the secrets of one of the greatest inventions of this century. Under pressure from Stafford Cripps and Harold Laski, the benevolent Labour Government of 1945 traded the Nene and Derwent jet engines with the Russians, which they copied and produced for their MiG-15 fighters, so giving parity with fighters used by the United Nations forces, including British, in the Korean War, 1950-53.

Power units for the great bomber aircraft of nations which developed strategic nuclear deterrent forces in the years after the war, were evolved from this British invention; an invention which has since contributed directly or indirectly to other methods of delivery that were devised in succeeding years. Nuclear weapons, also, owed much to British scientific genius and enterprise. Yet the first ten years after the war, so far as RAF Bomber Command was concerned, were distinguished only by depressing decisions that compelled aircrew to continue to fly old, piston-engined aircraft, despite rapid developments in jet propulsion in the United States and elsewhere, and to train in World War II bombing tactics.

It was not until 1952 that any visible sign of priority became evident in the production of new, long-range jet bombers, whose designs had been approved as far back as 1949. As early as 1944, a requirement for a light, twin-jet bomber had been issued by the Air Staff, but its performance characteristics were such that, even if it had become available in 1950, Bomber Command could still not have operated as a strategic, long-range strike force in either the nuclear or conventional role. The atomic bomb was not yet available, the range of the aircraft was too short and its bomb carrying capacity was less than half that of the Lincoln. But it was to prove to be a very important addition to Bomber Command's strike capability when it finally entered operational service in 1951. It was called the Canberra.

In January 1947, when the Air Staff issued an operational requirement for a more advanced four-jet bomber with greater strategic capabilities, it was recognized that it would probably take a minimum of eight years to develop; in the meantime Bomber Command would have to struggle on with Lincolns, at least through the fifties. So in August 1947, specifications for another jet bomber were issued to provide for "insurance aircraft", until the more advanced designs became available. The new aircraft later named Sperrin showed promise, but it was not destined to play a part in re-equipping Bomber Command. Re-equipment with modern jet aircraft was, however, in sight. The first Canberra was soon to start flying trials and the Command appeared to be embarking, in a modest way, on the long journey taking it in stages along the difficult road to its ultimate goal of creating a nuclear strike force and eventually an independent nuclear deterrent. There were many obstacles still to be overcome, not only those of a political and economic nature but from within the Services.

The year 1948 provided a good example of the sort of opposition that was to be encountered from time to time during the creation and deployment of the British independent nuclear strike force. A small, but vocal, minority had for some time been advancing the familiar argument that Britain should relinquish all claims to a bomber force and leave strategic air operations to the United States. They did not, initially, appear to command much support among the rest of the community. Nevertheless, men in responsible positions felt bound to draw attention to the consequences of opting out of the strategic strike role and sacrificing our ability to pose a nuclear deterrent or deliver nuclear or conventional weapons from the air in war. Among those voicing their opinions fearlessly and potently was Air Marshal Sir John Slessor, then Commandant of the Imperial Defence College. In 1949, he wrote an article for *The Sunday Times* drawing attention to the dangers of the policy being advocated by this small but politically influential minority. The substance of his article was as follows:

"A theory is gaining ground to the effect that heavy bombers are today so expensive that we should leave all long-range strategic bombing to the Americans and ourselves concentrate on home defence fighters, maritime squadrons for the protection of trade, and tactical air forces to co-operate with the Army ...

"To suggest that the RAF should, so to speak, go out of business in the long-range bomber trade altogether is in my view dangerously unsound. I think this idea is partly due to a failure to understand what allied bombing actually did do last time, how much we owe to them, not only for the ultimate victory but for our own relative immunity from air attack. Its crucially important contribution to Germany's defeat by drying up her oil, paralysing her transportation and bringing her war economy to a grinding halt in the last twelve months of the war has been obscured by the smoke-screen of irrelevant battle between extremists. And far to few people in the services, let alone in civil life, have any idea of the extent to which we owed the almost incredible degree of air superiority that we enjoyed from about Alamein onwards to the fact that the air war was fought over the Reich and not over the land or sea battle fields ...

"There is a great deal to be said for two very experienced and technically accomplished nations like ourselves and the United States going ahead on parallel but different lines of development towards a common goal, the ability to put a bomb where you want it against opposition. In the last war we and the Americans learned an immense amount from each other in the spheres of tactics and techniques; and the bomber forces working one by day and the other by night each in his own way, maintained that all-round-the-clock bombing which put such an intolerable strain on the enemy defences ...

"We must have our own striking force, much smaller but making up by the excellence of its quality for the relative numerical weakness. Only so can we be sure of having immediately available the punch that we might desperately need for purposes such as those I have described and (most important) only so can we earn the right to have any say whatever in the direction of the allied strategic bomber offensive of which the effects might be of such literally vital concern to us as a nation."

Despite the actions of disruptive elements the development of Britain's nuclear bomber force went ahead entirely independently of America, but in a spirit of friendly co-operation and mutual respect between Bomber Command and the United States Strategic Air Command. The problems confronting both forces in those early days were similar, though the Americans were well in advance in the development of aircraft and nuclear weapons.

In 1949, projects being studied by the aircraft industry in response to Air Ministry specifications for a new four-engine jet bomber reached a point where firm proposals to meet Air Staff requirements were submitted by Vickers, Handley Page and Avro and were examined in great detail by the Air Staff. All three appeared to be of excellent design and met the required operational specifications, though the time scale for production came as something of a shock, especially for the more advanced designs submitted by Handley Page and Avro. After much deliberation, the Air Council (which by then had Air Chief Marshal Sir John Slessor as its Chief of the Air Staff) decided to order all three types. It was a very courageous decision, for there were few precedents for such action in the annals of the Royal Air Force. If the Treasury had been parsimonious and forced a decision on one type only, the choice would have been difficult. It is just possible as events turned out that the wrong one could have been chosen.

The Vickers design, the Valiant, was to be produced first on high priority as an interim aircraft in place of the Sperrin; the other two were to follow as quickly as possible. The wisdom of this decision was revealed many years later. The Valiant was a medium-range aircraft of high performance, but less sophisticated than the other two. If it had not been decided to produce the Valiant at top priority in 1949, there would have been no suitable aircraft from which to drop Britain's first operational nuclear weapon at the test range at Maralinga in 1956, or the first thermonuclear weapon at Christmas Island in 1957.

The earlier proposal for a four-jet aircraft (the Short Sperrin) as an "insurance bomber", considered by the Air Staff in 1947, resulted in a design for an aircraft with a performance well below that of the Valiant, but it did offer the desirable prospect of providing Bomber Command with a long-range, strategic capability at an earlier date. When the Valiant was given top priority, production of the Sperrin could no longer be justified and its development as a bomber was cancelled. Fortunately, the aircraft had only reached the prototype stage and by that time it was already clear that it could not have been produced all that much faster than the Valiant.

The Avro proposal was a more advanced design for a high-performance four-engined jet bomber, incorporating a delta-wing structure and other new features. Its range and load carrying capacity were far greater than anything previously operated by the RAF in any role, and appropriately enough it was called the Vulcan. Handley Page's design, the Victor, was equally impressive. This was a crescent-wing concept, not previously used in any bomber design, and its performance also fully met Air Staff requirements. A choice between these two would have been extremely difficult, but fortunately both were ordered and world beaters they proved to be. The Valiant, Vulcan and Victor inevitably became known as the "V-bombers".

But to return for a moment to the realities of the fifties. The US Military Aid Programme, launched in 1949 to help free nations of the world to fortify their defences against the growing menace of Communism, offered a variety of aircraft, including bombers, in a wide range of military equipment. The bombers were Boeing B-29 Superfortresses, similar to those serving with Strategic Air Command of the United States Air Force, some of whose squadrons were based in Britain. The offer was accepted by the British Government and early in 1950 the first B-29s arrived in Bomber Command. Named the Washington in RAF service they were a welcome addition to its strike capability and far superior to the Lincolns equipping most of the squadrons. Although piston-engined aircraft, their cruising speed was over 300 mph; they had a ceiling of between 30,000 and 35,000 feet and a range of about 3,500 miles. Morale among bomber crews improved considerably when they were re-equipped with these fine aircraft and it was obvious even to the most naïve observers that they could carry nuclear weapons. The American aircraft based in Britain were already carrying them, although this was not generally known at the time.

Opinion in this country, both inside and outside the Services, was divided on the wisdom of relying on American aircraft and equipment for strategic bombing requirements, despite the obvious advantages of Bomber Command flying the same aircraft types as Strategic Air Command, instead of struggling along with outdated Lincolns which impressed no one, least of all the aircrews who flew them. (Our American colleagues referred to the Lincolns affectionately as "Abrahams".) There was also considerable controversy over the general pattern of future defence requirements which acceptance of these aircraft might dictate. Some argued that there was a danger of Britain's own new designs, which had created such a favourable impression, being cancelled and a policy of buying off-the-shelf substituted. This would have meant a severe reduction in aeronautical research and development which had made such a massive contribution to world aviation, in addition to the adverse economic effects it would undoubtedly have had on the British aircraft industry. These fears were eventually dispelled and production of the V-bombers went ahead, but it is remarkable how this predicament has repeatedly arisen in the development of air power in this country and was evident once again in 1965, alas with disastrous results, when the TSR-2 was cancelled in favour of the United States F-111, which was also cancelled three months later.

Another sharp controversy which developed in the 'fifties and has since recurred, was the question of defence against nuclear attack. The tremendously destructive power of nuclear weapons created a feeling of despair and helplessness in the minds of most people who thought about the subject rationally. There was a large body of opinion advocating that high priority should be accorded to producing fighters to ward off any attempt to bomb these islands with nuclear weapons; another faction proclaimed that nuclear weapons were so terrible that nothing could, or should, be done in defence against them. One could fully appreciate the anxiety felt by government and other public bodies for the safety and security of the population, and their desire to provide the most effective defences possible, active and passive, civil and military. But a policy of fighters only, or any other defensive weapons system as the only protection against nuclear attack, would have been utterly futile then, as it would be today and probably always will be.

Few people in the early 'fifties had seen the effects of nuclear weapons or appreciated the hard truth that interception and destruction of all bombers sent against this country in a nuclear attack would have been virtually impossible. Even if a 90 per cent destruction rate could have been guaranteed, and only twenty out of two hundred bombers had penetrated into densely populated areas in the Midlands and home counties, destruction would have been wrought on an unprecedented scale. Today there are weapons two thousand times more powerful than the nominal kiloton bombs of the late 'forties, but the lessons of history have apparently still to be learnt. In civil and military circles in this country and on the continent, one continues to hear people advocating a policy of concentrating our resources on air defence for the protection of these islands and of Europe, leaving all offensive air action, nuclear or conventional, to the Americans. These people do not appear to understand that the defence organization necessary to provide total protection for these islands against manned aircraft or missiles is technically unobtainable, and even if it could be produced, it would be beyond our economic resources. Yet in 1951, the Parliamentary Under-Secretary of State for Air, Aidan Crawley, told the House of Commons that "Air defence of this country is the most vital factor in our defence". He was not alone in this misconception of the use of air power.

Sir John Slessor, Lord Trenchard and others had pointed out in numerous documents the overwhelming contribution to victory made by long-range strike aircraft in the last war; how they won air superiority over Europe in the critical years after 1940 and allowed our own air power to operate relatively unhindered, especially in support of allied armies in the later stages of the reconquest of Europe. But some people found it hard to accept that the days of the Battle of Britain were over; no longer would knights in Hurricanes and Spitfires – or even Lightnings – sweep the skies clear of enemy marauders, to the adulation of an incredulous civilian population. They were great days while they lasted, but they were of short duration.

In 1940, battles in the air followed much the same pattern as they had done in the war of 1914-18, and it was hardly surprising that the results showed a similar trend. But from 1940 onwards, war in the air took on a new look and the final outcome revealed that Germany made a cardinal error in concentrating on fighters and anti-aircraft guns for defence of the Reich, at the expense of bombers. The Germans struggled for mastery in the skies over Europe with a vast armada of defensive fighters, searchlights, anti-aircraft artillery and radar, in a vain attempt to protect their homeland from the British and American bomber offensive. Meanwhile, they neglected to provide a long-range strike force until it was too late. If the V2 weapon had arrived two years earlier, it might have made a great deal of difference to Germany – and to us.

There was a danger in the early fifties, therefore, that we might again become so engrossed in the pursuit of air defence at all costs, that other considerations would be subordinated to this single aim. Indeed, at one time during the Korean War of 1950-53, top priority was accorded to fighters, though mercifully, not at the expense of the V-bombers. This policy had one favourable side effect in that it demanded more rapid development of jet engines, and ensured that some of the finest engines in the world were available for the new jet bombers when they did finally emerge.

As related, the first jet bomber to enter service with Bomber Command was the twin-engined Canberra. Few could have foreseen what a fine aircraft it would turn out to be and the very important role it was destined to play in British nuclear tests. The prototype first flew on 13th May 1949 and showed great promise. With further development, the aircraft proved so versatile that it was utilized in almost every role except that of interceptor fighter, in almost every theatre of operations in the world, for more than two decades. The pace of development of the V-bombers had been disappointingly slow and the introduction of the Canberra, despite its limitations, became pressing. By 1951 they began to reach the operational squadrons and provided an excellent intermediate jet bomber and training aircraft as a preliminary to the V-bombers which, alas, did not arrive in the operational squadrons until four years later. The introduction of the Canberra also gave a much needed boost to morale in Bomber Command, and by the end of 1954 nearly every squadron in the

43

Command was equipped with them; the Lincolns went and so, too, did the B-29 Washingtons.

The outbreak of the Korean War in 1950 frightened the Labour Government into a rearmament programme which Attlee told the House of Commons would cost about £3 billion over a three-year period. NATO, only recently formed, had neither an effective military command structure nor sufficient armed forces for the defence of Western Europe against attack from the east. Since both China and the Soviet Union were involved in the Korean War, the Chinese providing the manpower and the Russians the weapons and equipment, there was a genuine fear that the conflict might escalate into World War III.

The major share of the rearmament programme was to be devoted to air defence with orders for a large number of fighters, but with a small increase of Canberras as well. There was dissension and division in the Labour Party and in the government, and doubts in the Conservative opposition, about the ability of the aircraft industry to meet the heavy demands being placed on it in the time scale laid down. The RAF was in no position to undertake an expansion programme following so soon after the massive run-down between 1946 and 1949. The V-bombers had been ordered, but there was no way that production could be speeded. In the political and economic climate prevailing in 1951, the country decided to return a Conservative Government at the general election. This was fortunate for the country and for the RAF, since the re-election of another Labour Government might have increased the possibility that the V-bomber programme would have been cancelled. Too many of Attlee's government were against rearmament and the creation of a nuclear deterrent. Bevan and Wilson were among those who protested loudly at the priority given to rearmament at the expense of social services in April 1951, and as a result they resigned from the Cabinet.

With Churchill back in power, a reappraisal of the state of the country's economy, the ability of the aircraft industry to meet the programme drawn up by the Labour Government and the RAF's capacity to expand, showed that the programme was over-ambitious and could not be met. In slowing down the programme, Churchill said that Britain would have to rely on the United States for her security and on "the atom bomb to provide a deterrent against aggression during the period of forming a defensive front in Europe". In 1952, the government announced cut-backs in fighter production and in the number of Canberras on order, but no reduction or slowing down in V-bomber programmes.

In the United States, although there had been a very considerable rearmament programme to meet the demands of the Korean War, especially after the entry of China as an active participant, the Eisenhower administration was thinking in terms of nuclear deterrence to global war as the primary and overriding strategy in future defence policy. Following the successful test of a thermonuclear weapon in the Pacific in 1954, the results of which astounded even those scientists who had predicted that the explosive force would be a thousand times more powerful than the bomb that destroyed Hiroshima, the nuclear deterrent strategy of "massive retaliation" was adopted.

Churchill and the Conservative Government decided to press ahead with the production of nuclear weapons, the V-bomber force and the formation of an independent British nuclear deterrent and to adopt a similar strategy. This decision was welcomed by the vast majority of the British people and opposed only by those whose priorities and loyalty were already suspect.

The Valiant made its maiden flight in 1951, but suffered a setback when the prototype was destroyed in a crash on 12th January 1952. Fortunately, the second aircraft was nearing completion and took to the air on 11th April 1952, so that the test programmes did not suffer major interruptions. Despite this, the first production aircraft did not fly until late 1953 and it was not until 1955 that Bomber Command received the first operational aircraft at RAF Wittering. By this time scientists at the Atomic Weapons Research Establishment at Aldermaston had produced the prototype of a small operational nuclear weapon suitable for carriage on an aircraft, but in retrospect it seems reasonable to suggest that progress on both programmes should have been better. This is not a reflection on our scientific staffs or on industry; it was the system of procurement and production that was wrong.

The first Vulcan prototype made its debut in August 1952, but was disappointing in performance. A year later, fitted with more powerful engines, the second prototype was tested with very encouraging results. The first production aircraft came off the line in February 1955. The Victor followed a similar pattern. The first prototype flew on Christmas Eve 1952, but unfortunately it was destroyed in an accident while undergoing trials. The second prototype flew in September 1954 and the first production aircraft was delivered in February 1956. All three types were behind scheduled delivery dates and the Mk 2 versions of the Vulcan and Victor took even longer. Re-equipment of the Command with new jet bombers capable of long-range strategic operations took five years to complete from the time the first Valiant came into service with No138 squadron in 1955, until the last Victor Mk 1 arrived in 1960. The first operational Vulcan squadron, No83, was formed in 1957 and the first Victor squadron, No10, in 1958.

It was fortunate for Bomber Command during those sombre years that men like Air Marshal Sir Hugh Pugh Lloyd were still serving in the Royal Air Force. In 1950 Sir Hugh, appointed Commander-in-Chief Bomber Command, immediately set about regenerating some of the old life and spirit into what had once been a great force, but which had become despondent at the slow rate of re-equipment with new jet aircraft. His inaugural conference, appropriately named "Mimosa", set a pattern for the future. It projected Bomber Command into the jet and nuclear age, and prepared it for its major role in Britain's defence policy over the next two decades. It was fortunate, too, that United States Air Force B-29 squadrons were based on RAF Bomber Command airfields. There was a constant exchange of information between Bomber Command and Strategic Air Command on tactics and operating procedures which was of inestimable value in keeping Bomber Command's knowledge abreast of developments both in Britain and America; but, not unnaturally, discussions on nuclear weapons were strictly limited, even though the B-29s carried them, they were stored on Bomber Command airfields, and the RAF had some knowledge of their effects and the operating techniques.

The early 'fifties saw slow but methodical progress in Britain's efforts to create an independent nuclear deterrent. Scientists had already designed and tested two nuclear devices, and new jet aircraft were in production, to give Bomber Command a real strategic capability. But aircraft alone could not provide the means of delivery for nuclear weapons in the highly scientific and technological age which had so recently dawned. In 1953, a special cell was established within the Directorate of Bomber Operations in the Air Ministry with responsibility for the formulation of policy covering the training and operation of the embryo nuclear force, deciding on the range and types of equipment needed to enable it to operate successfully in all weathers, devising tactics and training facilities required at the operational training units to meet an intensive and complicated training programme when the new aircraft appeared. This involved the provision of navigation and bombing aids, electronic devices, armament equipment (including special handling and storage facilities for nuclear weapons), ground and air control systems to ensure that the new and very expensive aircraft could operate safely from home and overseas bases, and a host of other related items.

The unrivalled knowledge Bomber Command had amassed during the war years was readily available in various Air Ministry branches, together with individual experiences, were invaluable in the formative years of the independent nuclear deterrent. The art of blind bombing was to become once again very much a part of Bomber Command's training and operational techniques. H2S blind bombing equipment, designed and used to good effect during the war, had to be redesigned, improved in performance and produced in quantity to enable each aircraft to be self-sufficient in navigation and bombing, and to penetrate enemy defences. The old concept of a special force of Pathfinders to find and mark targets for others to bomb was no longer valid. The days of the thousand-bomber raids were over. Nuclear weapons capable of destroying whole cities had made wartime tactics in these respects obsolete, but many of the principles governing successful strategic bombing operations still applied.

It was clear that the new aircraft would have to fly further to attack targets in potential enemy territory, and with improvements in enemy defences they would have to fly higher and faster as well. Navigation and bombing aids would have to be completely independent of ground aids, and at the great heights the new aircraft were designed to fly, visual identification of targets would rarely be possible. Wartime efforts at degrading enemy ground and air defences by radio and radar counter-measures, as they were called, though effective in 1945 were clearly not going to be good enough in any future conflict. A great deal of research and development was needed to produce more elaborate and effective electronics for the V-bombers if it were again decided to adopt a policy of evasion as the primary means of ensuring the safety of the force. One of the major difficulties at this time was to decide what equipment to design. An enemy's defensive system can be countered successfully only when it is known what it consists of and how it is deployed, and no Air Defence Commander wittingly reveals his methods of intercepting and destroying enemy aircraft. Britain was a pioneer in the electronic counter-measures (ECM) field, as in so many others, and a scientific organization able to carry out research into ways and means of producing the equipment likely to be needed for future operations already existed within the Air Ministry.

Perhaps the most difficult problem, and certainly the most controversial, was to decide whether the new generation of V-bombers should carry defensive armament and if so of what kind. Alternatively, as in earlier days, reliance could be placed on speed and other performance factors, supplemented by electronic counter-measures to ensure the safety of the aircraft. It was evident that future tactics would preclude flying in large gaggles, concentrated in time and space by accurate navigation, with all aircraft attacking the same target. It was also clear that Bomber Command would have to be prepared to operate by day or night; they had always been trained to do both, but there was still, at that time, an advantage to be gained by flying at night. In the last war, British bombers had been forced to adopt night operations; mainly because they did not have escort fighters, the bombers were lightly armed, and could not survive against enemy day fighters. The Americans, on the other hand, decided as a matter of policy that they would operate by day and rely on heavily armed gun turrets mounted in their bombers flying in tight formation. But operating in daylight from bases in this country against targets in Germany did not prove feasible until long-range escort fighters were introduced. Such tactics appeared to be outdated in the nuclear age.

It was inevitable, therefore, that when operational requirements for equipment in the V-bombers came to be discussed, there was considerable divergence of opinion on armament and armour. There were many interesting and helpful discussions with American experts on likely developments in enemy defence systems and the best tactics for overcoming them, but complete agreement was not possible on all aspects of the problem. The Americans initially appeared to favour daylight formation attacks for which, naturally, they proposed fitting guns to their aircraft. The RAF felt that the concept of large formations of bombers armed with nuclear weapons was totally obsolete in the nuclear age, and that any formation flying in future wars would only be possible over a portion of the route to the target. Sooner or later, aircraft would have to diverge to attack their allotted targets individually. Only one or two aircraft at most would be required on each target, and it did not seem possible that fighter escort could be provided over the enormous distances that would have to be traversed in any future war. Even flight refuelling, then in its infancy, did not seem to offer a solution to the problem of providing escort fighters for a large bombing force. In any event, this country was slow to implement in-flight refuelling − a system demonstrated many times over the years as an effective means of increasing range.

The disparity in speed and ceiling of jet fighters and jet bombers in the early 'fifties was small, and the RAF believed that the speed and height characteristics likely to be available in their new jet bombers, coupled with an elaborate array of equipment to provide extensive jamming and deception tactics *en route* to the target, would guarantee a reasonable degree of safety for the bombers. The Russians had never really understood the proper role of air power in World War II. They did not appear to appreciate the potentialities of strategic air power and consequently their aircraft were employed almost exclusively in close support of their armies and navies. They did not have a strategic bomber force comparable in performance with Bomber Command or the US 8th and 20th Air Forces, and their fighter force did not have an effective radar network for early warning and controlled inter-ceptions. It is a matter for speculation what might have happened if they had developed an efficient, long-range strike capability early in the war and had been in a position to launch a strategic air offensive against Germany from the east, in co-operation with Anglo-American strikes from the west. Apart from the effects which such an offensive might have had on German industry and morale, it is quite certain that it would have relieved some of the pressure on the Russian armies fighting for survival on their own soil.

But conditions in Russia had, of course, improved after 1945. They had received British Nene and Derwent jet engines at the end of the war and had made full use of them, both as power units for the first generation of their new jet aircraft and as a starting point to develop their own jet engine industry. Products from their factories in the years since Britain gave them jet engine technology have come to be regarded as of the highest quality, and in the 'fifties they embarked on a massive programme to produce a national air defence organization which became known as PVO Strany. Their progress in rocket engine design and space exploration has been no less remarkable.

A modern fighter defence system in the 'fifties, however good the performance of its aircraft, needed an elaborate radar network for early warning, tracking the bomber and close control of friendly fighters during interceptions. Looking at a map of Russia, it is evident that the Soviets face an enormous air defence problem. The frontier from Murmansk in the north to Odessa in the south is 1,350 miles. In the late 'fifties, it could be penetrated at almost any point by V-bombers with a high degree of safety. It could also be outflanked to the north and south. To provide complete air defence along the whole frontier in depth, was then a well-nigh impossible task, and this was an important factor to be considered in dealing with conflicting claims for the type of equipment to be provided for the V-bombers. Eventually it was decided that heavy armament would be unacceptable and the bombers would rely on their performance at high level, evasion and deception, as the basis of future tactics. This meant a determined effort in radio and radar counter-measures research, which presented a formidable scientific and technological task.

Once again the inventive genius of British scientists and the wartime experiences of bomber crews helped to direct designers along the right path in deciding the type of equipment needed for the new strategic bomber force. Britain had pioneered radio, radar and electronic countermeasures techniques and equipment during World War II, and had a head start on other countries in developing the more sophisticated deception appliances required in the jet and nuclear age. Many of the principles of "the war in the ether" had not changed, even if the instruments and methods of employing them had become more complicated. From 1953 onwards, a concerted effort was made to update electronic counter-measures doctrine, devise new designs and forecast likely developments in defence systems several years ahead, so that counter-measures could be ready if and when they were required. This was perhaps the most difficult aspect of planning the offensive air strike requirements for the V-bomber force. Other aspects, no less important, did not contain the element of guesswork necessary in forecasting likely trends associated with electronic counter-measures.

By 1954, the many and varied components of the nuclear deterrent force were in production, including aircraft, weapons, a wide range of complicated radio and radar equipment, bombing and navigation aids and electronic counter-measures devices. Progress was not spectacular, but the superior quality was already apparent, and there were solid grounds for optimism that the future of Bomber Command as Britain's independent nuclear deterrent was assured. This feeling of optimism was further encouraged when the United States Air Force invited Bomber Command to send a detachment of Canberra aircraft to the Pacific to take part in one of their thermonuclear, or H-bomb, tests at Einewetok. Soon afterwards this was followed by an invitation from the US Atomic Energy Commission for a party of officers from the Services and scientists from Aldermaston to visit the United States continental testing ranges in Nevada. This was a splendid gesture by the Americans and provided an ideal opportunity for British observers to see at first hand how they conducted their nuclear tests. The British series, which it was hoped to mount in 1956 or 1957, were already in the preliminary planning stages and the Nevada operations provided those responsible for the planning and conduct of the British tests with much valuable information.

4

The Nevada Tests

Nuclear weapons tests at the United States special range in the Nevada desert had become commonplace by 1955. Invited observers from a wide variety of interests throughout the United States had been able to witness many tests, and on at least one occasion a nuclear explosion was televised for public viewing in addition to the extensive coverage given to it by a large assembly of newsmen. Some of the explosions could, of course, be observed from outside the test site, merely by choosing a vantage point on one of the surrounding hills. If the tests happened to be air drops, they could be seen over a wide area, and provided visitors and local inhabitants with a spectacular and interesting display to distract their attention from the more fleshy entertainments to be had in the enchanting city of Las Vegas.

Among those attending the 1955 series was Sir William Penney, who, in addition to observing various tests, was able to renew his acquaintance with eminent American scientists from Los Alamos and other establishments, where he was well known and held in high esteem.

Details of the weapons to be tested were, of course, secret, but Staff briefings and Press releases by the authorities gave enough information for observers to understand the purpose of the tests, how they were being conducted, and the reasons for the strict safety regulations which had to be obeyed by everyone concerned with them. These regulations were designed to protect life and property from the effects of nuclear weapons and made testing on the American mainland safe and effective. The nuclear test area lies about 70 miles from Las Vegas, situated between two natural basins at some 4,000 feet surrounded by mountains rising to over 7,000 feet. The northern basin, called Yucca Flat, is separated from the southern, known as Frenchman's Flat, by French Mountain. Highway 95 from Las Vegas to Tonopan, passes within five miles of the entrance to the test site at Camp Desert Rock. Camp Mercury at the southern end of the range provides accommodation for test personnel, both civil and military. The Scientific Director of the series to which British observers had been invited was Dr Alvin C. Graves of the Los Alamos laboratories, and the Task Force Commander was General Strahathan of the United States Air Force, both of whom were later to visit Australia to watch some of the tests in Britain's second series at Maralinga in South Australia.

There was also a test manager, Mr James Reeves, who was responsible for all participating agencies, such as contractors' working parties, within the test site. Colonel Parsons, who was Deputy Military Commander and Director of Weapons Effects, gave a full and lucid briefing before each test, including details of the scope, type of weapon and safety regulations to be observed both before and after the explosion. These were particularly rigid for those who entered the test site after a shot had been fired.

All nuclear weapons release energy in four categories – light, heat, blast and nuclear radiation. Light is radiated in the form of a vivid flash seen at the instant of detonation. It is much brighter than the sun and dangerous to the eyes if viewed directly from close range. Permanent injury to the retina can result from looking directly at a nuclear burst, but protection can usually be guaranteed by wearing very dark glasses and not looking directly at the point of burst. Even a few degrees off is sufficient at a safe range. Heat is released instantaneously and can be felt on exposed parts of the body, such as the hands and face, as the hot gases expand and spread outwards from the centre of the explosion. This causes a shock wave, which, because of the high overpressures associated with it, is capable of damaging even the most solid structures by blast effect, the extent of which depends on the distance from "ground zero", as the point of burst is more commonly called.

Immediate nuclear radiation occurs at the instant of detonation, in the form of neutrons, accompanied by alpha, beta and gamma rays, as fission takes place. Residual radiation is emitted over a period of time from radioactive fission products and debris from the explosion. This occurs in the form of fall-out from the radioactive cloud which forms soon after detonation.

Within thousandths of a second after detonation, a fireball forms as the air surrounding the centre of the explosion becomes heated to incandescence. The size of the fireball depends upon the yield of the weapon, and for a 20-kiloton yield weapon reaches its maximum (usually several hundred feet) about one second after detonation. The shock wave, which produces blast effects, is visible as it spreads outwards ahead of the fireball and resembles a heat haze. About ten seconds after detonation, the fireball begins to cool and the radioactive cloud begins to ascend. By now the shock wave will have travelled about two miles, during which it would have destroyed most structures within a radius of one mile from ground zero, and severely damaged others up to a distance of two miles. At this point, the characteristic mushroom cloud is well defined, as the ascending gases cool down. The cloud contains debris from the weapon in the form of vaporized particles of the bomb casing and, if the weapon has been fired close to the ground, so that the fireball touches the surface, will also contain dirt and other debris sucked up by the intensity of the explosion. All this material will be radioactive and as the cloud begins to drift away from the test site, some of the radioactive particles will be deposited over an area down-wind of the test site. Most of the heavy particles will fall in the test area and from weapons of about 20 Kt or less there is very little hazard outside the immediate boundary of the test site. Phenomena associated with nuclear explosions are predictable and follow a regular pattern, but the intensity of three of the main features, heat, blast and nuclear radiation, increases in proportion to the yield of the weapon, each category according to a certain mathematical formula.

Thermonuclear, or megaton, weapons produce effects which are so much greater than atomic bombs that it is not possible to test them with safety near inhabited areas, and the higher the yield, the greater the hazards. This was amply demonstrated and widely publicized following American tests in the Pacific in 1954. It is clear, therefore, that there must be a strict limit to the yield of weapon that could be tested at the Nevada range, or at any other test site close to human habitation. Safety regulations were no less stringent whatever the yield of weapon being tested.

In order to guarantee full protection from flash during the Nevada tests, it was mandatory to stand with one's back to the explosion for at least three seconds after detonation, and to wear dark glasses. It was equally important to be sufficiently far from the centre of the explosion to escape the effects of blast. When these two conditions were fulfilled, there was no danger from immediate radiation, which is localized. Residual radiation, emitted by particles of radioactive debris falling from the cloud, was also localized, though over a fairly large area. Complete protection was assured by locating observers up-wind of the point of detonation. Wind direction and speed at the time of detonation plays an important part in planning any nuclear explosion and is the factor, more than any other, that can cause delays and postponements. Man still cannot control the elements but, while it is possible to forecast what the weather is likely to be on a particular day, such forecasts are not infallible. Another important factor worth stressing is that if a weapon is exploded on or near the ground, so that the fireball is in contact with the surface, resultant fall-out from the radioactive cloud will be greater than if it had been exploded high in the air. The importance of this will be apparent when the problems confronting those responsible for planning and mounting British thermonuclear tests in the Pacific in 1957 are discussed.

The security regulations at Nevada were of particular interest to all those attending the tests. The organization to implement them presented the authorities with quite a problem, especially as a main highway passed within five miles of the entrance to the test site. But they were always able to inform local inhabitants and passing travellers when a shot was due to be fired and advise them on precautions to be taken to safeguard health and property. The 1955 series was designed to follow the pattern of previous tests in that "weapons effects" was their principal object. In this series a high altitude burst was included, in addition to four explosions from steel towers. The largest of the tower shots was designed specifically to study the effects of nuclear weapons from both military and civil defence aspects, and many representatives from the United States Armed Forces, Civil Defence Organizations and Government

Departments were present to witness the test and examine the results. Another important aspect of this series was the indoctrination of aircrews who, although not otherwise involved in the tests, were permitted to fly in the vicinity of the test site and simulate nuclear attacks from the air.

A large and varied array of equipment from dummy soldiers in dugouts to fully furnished houses were a common feature at most tests, since useful information could always be obtained from any nuclear explosion and, in those early days, there was a constant demand for confirmation of existing data and for new measurements not previously recorded. All the tests followed a similar pattern, even when the primary objects were different, so it is only necessary to describe two shots; one exploded on a tower and one dropped from an aircraft at high altitude. The higher the yield of weapon exploded, of course, the more spectacular the display.

The air drop, in which a relatively small yield weapon was fused to burst at high altitude was first on the programme. The aiming point was high above Frenchman's Flat and, as the test had been widely publicized, a large and expectant crowd had taken up positions along Highway 95 near the test site, in order to view the display. Many were enjoying a picnic breakfast and there were no marchers or demonstrators (the Americans are a very realistic people!).

Thirty seconds before the weapon was due to be exploded, a B-47 Stratojet bomber, leading a formation of F-86 Sabres in line abreast, flew over the target zone on a north-westerly heading. They laid long lines of coloured smoke through an area of sky in which the bomb was expected to burst, and dropped clusters of flares and containers fitted with measuring instruments suspended from parachutes. The object was to record the effects of the burst for possible application as a form of defence against high flying enemy aircraft. At zero hour, a B-36, flying at about 30,000 feet, passed over the range and sighted the bomb on the flare clusters. A few seconds later there was a vivid flash, whitish blue and much brighter than the sun, which quickly turned to golden red as the fireball developed. But it lasted only a few seconds, the intense cold at the height at which the weapon had exploded cooled the fireball very quickly and, instead of a mushroom cloud, a perfectly formed smoke-ring appeared, lasted for several minutes and then drifted away on the strong upper winds. The blast wave was clearly audible as it reached ground level, but the effect was insignificant. The special containers, whose parachutes were designed to lower them to the ground at different speeds, slowly descended and, as they reached the surface, members of the scientific staff were there to collect them and begin the important task of analysing the recorded measurements. It was not a particularly exciting display, mainly because it took place a long way from the observers' viewing point. There were no problems with fall-out, or, indeed, with any of the other effects associated with nuclear explosions.

The next test involved the explosion of a high yield weapon on top of a 400-foot steel tower on Frenchman's Flat. The primary object of the trial was to obtain information on weapons effects for the United States Department of Defense and the Civil Defence organizations. In all, some forty military effects tests were planned, and an impressive array of equipment, including tanks, troop carriers, jeeps, tractors, bulldozers, and many other types of vehicles were placed at selected points around the range at varying distances from the tower. Concrete structures, bridges, dug-outs, slit trenches and many types of buildings were erected in positions where they would be subjected to the full force of the blast wave. A large assortment of clothing and fabrics were exposed to the effects of the thermal pulse, to measure how different materials reacted to the intense heat.

Three types of surfaces were specially prepared close to the base of the tower to record the effects of heat and blast on each. The first was an artificial lake, the second an asphalt strip resembling an airfield runway, and the third a natural earth road, prepared from material obtained from a dried-up salt-bed nearby. All three areas radiated outwards from ground zero and were fully instrumented. Finally, there was the usual elaborate system of instrumentation and cameras to measure and record heat, blast and radiation effects at varying distances from the tower.

More than a hundred aircraft were scheduled to take part in the test, including aircrews undergoing indoctrination and simulating bombing attacks with nuclear weapons. Three unmanned QF-80 drones, remotely controlled, were to be exposed to the effects of the explosion, to receive varying degrees of heat, blast and radiation. It was calculated beforehand that one would crash in the test site, but at least one of the remaining two would survive and be guided to a base for inspection.

As the shot was to take place on Frenchman's Flat, in a natural basin between mountain ranges, the flash would not be seen directly from the highway or from any part of the surrounding areas, but could be viewed by anyone who wished to climb a nearby mountain. For this reason, the usual warnings were broadcast throughout the previous day to people living in the district. Warnings were also broadcast on national radio networks. On this occasion, too, there were additional instructions on safety precautions for those who were to enter the test area soon after the explosion, when the level of radiation had fallen sufficiently to make it safe.

The sky above the test site was clear and bright blue. Nothing stirred and an eerie silence descended over the range prior to the start of the test. But not for long: the loud speaker system crackled into life with the news that the three drones had taken off from Indian Springs Air Force Base under remote control, and observers were able to see them being manoeuvred into their allotted positions on headings to take them over the precise area planned for them at the instant of detonation.

A few minutes before zero hour, the sky above seemed to throb with the sound of aircraft engines. High flying B-36 and B-47 aircraft simulated air attacks; others with a variety of photographic and measuring tasks to perform were also approaching their final positions. The precision with which this part of the test was conducted was immensely impressive.

At two minutes before zero hour observers were instructed to put on dark glasses, so dense that they almost excluded the bright morning sun, and at one minute the final call came over the loud speakers. Everyone turned their backs on the tower, which in less than sixty seconds would be vaporized by the intensity of the heat from the explosion. With ten seconds to go, the calm, clear voice of the controller came over the speakers. Ten, nine, eight, seven, six, five, four, three, two, one – a pause of a fraction of a second, and then a blinding flash of light, much brighter than the morning sun, lit up the entire countryside even when viewed through almost opaque glasses.

After three seconds observers removed their goggles and looked again towards the tower. So intent were they on gazing at the awe-inspiring spectacle before them, that they were taken completely by surprise when the shock wave arrived with a deafening crack. This was followed by a rumbling like thunder, as the sounds of the explosion reverberated among the mountains and valleys surrounding Frenchman's Flat. The heat from the thermal pulse had been felt on the back of the neck immediately fission took place, but it was momentary and soon forgotten.

The fireball formed a few second after detonation, and very soon the hot gases, expanding and rising, began to take on the familiar mushroom shape. Dust and debris sucked up by the violence of the explosion were combining to create a boiling, flaming, multicoloured mass: red, brown, yellow and black. The seething column rose rapidly to a height of twenty thousand feet or more, the stem, still in contact with the ground, swirled and changed shape and colour, as the plume rose higher. After about fifteen minutes the cloud had risen to well over 40,000 feet, the stem had begun to lift and break, and the whole mass, by now a dull brownish colour, began to drift away on the light winds far out over the Nevada desert.

One of the drones had been destroyed and one damaged, but the third landed safely at its base under remote control. Other aircraft were busy overhead taking various measurements and photographs, while units on the ground prepared to collect large numbers of recording instruments from specially selected points on the range.

Four hours elapsed before it was safe to enter the test area, but the level of radiation was still much too high to permit a close inspection of ground zero. There was nothing left of the steel tower but a heap of ashes, but there was much to see and study at other parts of the range, having first passed through a special radiological check point commanding the entrance to the test site. Here, observers were issued with white overalls, caps, gloves, boots and dust masks. They were also given small dosimeters for measuring the amount of radiation received during the period spent in the contaminated area.

Scientific guides constantly checked the level of radiation as observers moved around the range. This was a sensible precaution taken to ensure that no one accidentally strayed into an area where it might have been unhealthy. On the outer perimeter of the range, radiation was low, and the track taken by the guides in their jeeps followed a wide circular path, gradually converging towards the centre, as radiation levels permitted. The limit of radiation was set at about ten roentgens, which is quite safe for a brief period.

The effects of the explosion were everywhere evident. The ground was pockmarked and burnt, tanks, armoured personnel carriers and jeeps were almost totally destroyed. The jeeps, in particular, were ripped to pieces and debris was strewn over a wide area. It was a scene of unbelievable devastation extending to about a mile from ground zero. On the spot where the tower had stood, the ground was black and scarred; the sand round the base of the tower had been crystallized. The asphalt surface was still burning; an area of sand about two hundred yards in diameter had been fused into glass. Buildings and other steel structures within a mile of ground zero were destroyed, others were twisted out of all recognition. Clothing and fabrics had been burnt or scorched and timber buildings were still burning. This was caused by only a relatively small yield fission weapon, of about 15 kilotons; already, at Bikini Atoll in the Pacific, a new fusion weapon, more than two hundred times as powerful, had been successfully tested in 1954.

The most impressive aspect of the administrative arrangements for nuclear testing at the Nevada site was that the base organization for air and ground support was centred on an airfield only thirty-five miles from the test site, linked by road, rail and air communications with every important military and scientific centre in the United States. British tests were to be conducted in Australia, twelve thousand miles from home bases with only skeleton communications of any kind inside Australia. The logistic problems for British planners were clearly going to be formidable and air support was likely to be on a much greater scale than had been envisaged in the preliminary planning stages.

RAF officers attached to the Nevada test site and based at Indian Springs air force station were given every assistance and a great deal of valuable information that was to prove of immense help in planning and executing the British tests one year later. United States Air Force officers and scientists visited Australia and Christmas Island while

British tests were in progress, thus maintaining the tradition of friendship and mutual respect which the two Services have always had for each other. The Nevada test site was also to be an important factor in Britain's efforts to maintain a strategic nuclear force throughout the 1970s when no other test facilities were available anywhere in the world on which Britain could test her new or modified nuclear warheads.

5

Planning British Nuclear Tests

In the summer of 1955 the Ministry of Supply, the controlling and co-ordinating authority for British nuclear test programmes, launched a plan for the construction of a new atomic weapons testing range at Maralinga in South Australia, in agreement with, and co-operation from, the Australian Government. But before any official announcement could be made, a great deal of preliminary planning had to be completed. The programme, as envisaged in 1955, was to begin testing at Maralinga in the second half of 1956, the series to last about three months, during which four or five weapons in the kiloton range would be exploded. Maralinga, an aboriginal word meaning the place of thunder, lies about three hundred miles west of Adelaide and fifty miles north of a small town called Watson, on the trans-continental railway between Perth and Adelaide. Construction of the range, it was estimated, could not be finished before mid-1956 at the earliest, since the scope of the tests demanded a formidable organization and elaborate facilities.

The object, as stated by the Ministry, was "to carry out proof tests of nuclear weapons and to advance research and development". This was to include experiments in which measurements of nuclear weapons effects would be made, particularly those associated with blast and heat, on various structures and materials. Confirmation was also to be sought of the effects of immediate and residual radiation, which necessitated the inclusion of certain biological experiments in the programme. A committee, known as the Buffalex Committee, whose Chairman (General Sir Frederick Morgan) was the Controller of Atomic Weapons, Ministry of Supply, was set up to direct and co-ordinate the trials. Members were drawn from various bodies, including the three Service Ministries, the Treasury and the Atomic Weapons Research Establishment at Aldermaston. The Director of Trials was Sir William Penney and a Task Force Commander was to be appointed later, when planning was more advanced.

The scope of the trials, code-named Buffalo, outlined at the first meeting, clearly indicated that air support would be required on a large scale and embrace a variety of roles. One of the biggest demands would be for an airlift from the United Kingdom to Australia, and internally once the task force was established at its main base. Before any useful progress in planning air requirements could be made, it was necessary to discuss with Australian authorities various aspects of the proposed trials and the assistance that would be needed from their resources. The Buffalex Committee, therefore, approved a proposal that a team, consisting of representatives of the Royal Air Force, the Ministry of Supply and the Atomic Weapons Research Establishment, should visit Australia to review these problems. Their task was to inspect installations, communications and accommodation at selected airfields, including a base airfield, examine proposed installations at Maralinga and other sites and recommend what additional facilities, if any, should be provided to meet the requirements of the trials.

The team left London Airport on 26th May 1955, and arrived in Melbourne to conduct a rapid series of conferences with the Department of Supply, Department of Works, Civil Aviation Ministry and the Royal Australian Air Force. Excellent arrangements had been made by the Australian Department of Supply, under Mr O'Connor's direction, for most of the discussions to be held in his conference rooms in Swanson Street, and this saved a lot of time and effort.

During these talks, the scope of the nuclear tests, and how it was proposed to support them, were outlined to the Australian authorities. Initial plans were agreed for additional facilities at Maralinga, envisaged as the forward operating base for all types of aircraft, with Edinburgh Field, an RAAF station near Adelaide, as the main base. Other airfields, widely dispersed over the Australian continent, would also be needed for refuelling aircraft. Agreement on outline plans having been reached, the next step was to visit various establishments and discuss detailed proposals. A programme was quickly arranged by the Department of Supply and the RAAF, who had generously

An American underwater nuclear explosion at Bikini 1953.

Close-up of the atomic cloud formations after an explosion in the Monte Bello tests, 1952.

Boxes of vegetables, sweet corn, lettuce, tomatoes, melons etc, are placed in the vicinity of the explosion to discover how much radiation they will absorb. Similarly boxed and tinned foods are left to discover the effectiveness of containers as protection against contamination.

Admiral Mountbatten visits the Monte Bello test site.

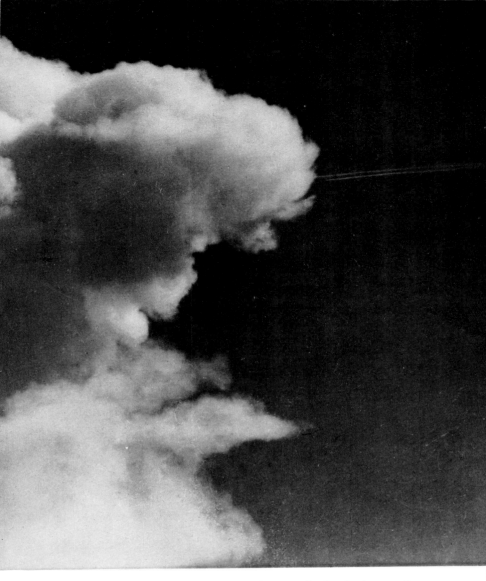

Vapour trails of Canberras seen approaching atomic cloud minutes after the explosion of the second test at Monte Bello.

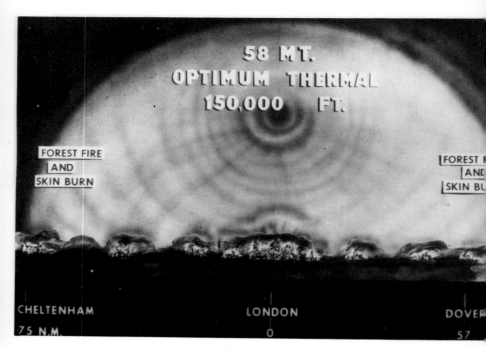

Thermal and blast effects of a 58-megaton bomb.

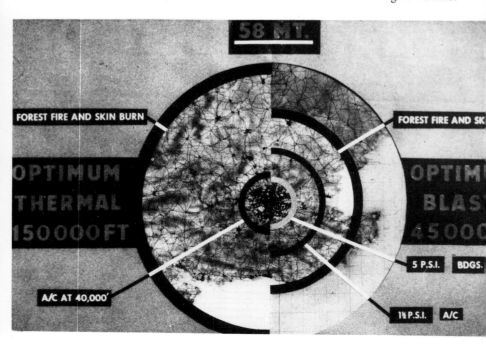

Sir William Penney with Air Commodore C.T. Weir and the author (left).

Air Vice-Marshal W.E. Oulton inspects a Fijian Guard of Honour on arrival at Christmas Island.

(*Opposite*) The renovated airstrip at Christmas Island seen from ground and air, showing a line-up of Canberra B2s and B6s in natural finish, two Valiants in white finish and Shackletons in white-topped maritime camouflage.

The thermonuclear cloud of a Megaton Bomb exploded high in the air, Christmas Island, 1957.

placed both air and road transport at the team's disposal. Before commencing their extensive tour, it was agreed that at the end of it the team should return to Melbourne to talk over a final joint plan and list recommendations.

The first visit was to Edinburgh Field, run jointly by the RAAF, the Australian Department of Supply and the British Ministry of Supply. This airfield supported rocket experimental activities at the test range at Woomera and a scientific establishment at Salisbury, about four miles from Adelaide. An inspection of the airfield quickly confirmed that it would make an ideal main base for operations and provide an excellent terminal for transport aircraft arriving from the United Kingdom, but it was already engaged on a busy flying programme supporting other projects under the auspices of the two Ministries and had little to spare in the way of buildings for technical or domestic accommodation. Parking space for aircraft was also fully occupied, but the RAAF offered their full co-operation.

Tentative proposals were made for additions to existing facilities at Edinburgh, including a new hangar, concrete standings for aircraft, workshops, communications centres, barracks and a hospital. Other, less expensive but equally necessary, items were also included. After three busy days at Edinburgh, the team set off in an RAAF DC-3 to visit Woomera and Maralinga.

Woomera, of course, had been in existence for many years as an experimental rocket range, and among its many assets was an excellent airfield capable of operating most types of modern jet aircraft. It offered good facilities as an advanced refuelling station and as a secondary maintenance base if, for any reason, Edinburgh Field should not be available. It was on a direct route from Darwin to Edinburgh, where RAF transport aircraft from Britain could stage once the build-up began.

To reach Maralinga involved a three-hour flight from Woomera over desolate, featureless terrain, covered with stunted trees and scrub struggling for survival in what appeared to be a waterless wasteland of reddish, sandy soil. Occasionally, a dried-up river bed or salt pan indicated that at times some rain must have fallen, but nowhere was there any sign of water or any living creature.

At this stage, Maralinga consisted of a small collection of tents clustered beside a bare strip of earth. This was a landing ground, which had been hacked out of the bush, bulldozed flat and then rolled to provide a reasonably smooth surface. It was good enough for a DC-3, but would not have taken anything larger. In any case, it was only a temporary strip until a new airfield could be built. To the north, west and east lay flat or gently undulating country, stretching as far as the eye could see, and in the clear, unpolluted air visibility was almost unlimited. To the south lay the Nullabor Plain, a hard, rocky, barren outcrop, covering hundreds of square miles. Through it, on a single track, ran the trans-continental railway from Perth, a thousand miles to the west, to Adelaide. One of many stopping places on this railway was a small station called Watson, fifty miles south of Maralinga and the only railhead which could provide an overland means of communication with the range. It was to become an important logistic link with Maralinga throughout the nuclear test programme.

The team's main interests centred on proposals for a new airfield and facilities for handling a considerable volume of air traffic of all kinds. The ground was reasonably flat and there were no approach obstructions for at least five hundred miles, so siting problems were not difficult to solve. The next task was to decide upon the best locations for buildings and fuel installations. This presented some minor difficulties, because bore holes were being sunk in several places in an attempt to find water, and it was important not to site fuel or oil storage tanks adjacent to the best water holes. Agreement was reached in less than a day and the team returned to Edinburgh Field.

There still remained the problem of establishing a communications network to connect Maralinga, Woomera, Edinburgh and a score of other airfields that might be needed by aircraft engaged on tracking and recording the paths of the radioactive clouds resulting from the tests. Some of these airfields were far removed from cities, or main centres of population, and bore romantic names reminiscent of pioneering days, like Alice Springs, Tennants Creek, Cloncurry, Broome and Wyndham. There was a great deal of planning still to be done, but at least the project was now launched and would gather momentum in the months ahead.

After two further meetings at Edinburgh Field with the RAAF and the Department of Supply, agreement was reached on the improvements and additional facilities needed at Edinburgh and Maralinga. Three more days were spent in Melbourne drawing up a final plan with the Australian authorities, who had been extremely helpful and co-operative throughout the visit. Financial considerations, fortunately, were not the team's direct responsibility, although in all deliberations cost usually dominated the proceedings. After two busy but productive weeks the team returned to London.

The next meeting of the Buffalex Committee approved the recommendations put forward by the team on its return from Australia, and forwarded them to the Treasury for approval and funding. But a new complication arose when it was decided that some preliminary tests should be conducted at the Monte Bello Islands before embarking on the Maralinga trials. This necessitated a further visit to Australia to discuss requirements for a preliminary series of tests in the islands.

The Monte Bello Islands lie about eighty miles off the north-west coast of Australia. The nearest habitation is a little port called Onslow, typical of Australian towns in that remote region – one street, what passes for a hotel and a few shops. There was little activity in the town in 1956 and, apart from a few aborigines, the inhabitants were mainly fishermen, and included some of the last of the pioneers and pearl fishers of a bygone era. The seas in that part of the world abound with fish, mostly sharks, and the long sea journey to the islands in rough weather was never a pleasant prospect. Helicopters were an obvious alternative form of transport, if only as a means of saving time, though the thought of flying over a shark-infested ocean several times a day, with only one engine, was unlikely to commend itself to either crews or passengers.

Onslow had a small sandy airstrip, visited frequently by aircraft of a local air transport company. It was also possible to land at several places on the beach. A small Royal Australian Naval Station provided radio communication with the outside world, but otherwise there were no facilities of any kind. A small jetty, used by coastal ships, offered some opportunity for loading and unloading heavy equipment and supplies destined for Onslow or the islands, all of which would have to be brought from Fremantle, 800 miles to the south, and the nearest suitable point of entry by sea from the United Kingdom. The main

67

problem was how to operate jet and piston-engined aircraft, including heavy transports, from a suitable main base as near the islands as possible. Transport from Fremantle, or the civil airport at Perth, would be necessary anyway, and helicopter lift from Onslow to the islands despite the difficulties, was essential. The tests were not going to be either elaborate or protracted, but it was estimated that a task group of about 350 officers and men would be required. This postulated that the main base for operations would have to be equipped with a minimum of buildings to provide living accommodation for the men and reasonable maintenance facilities for the aircraft.

There were no such facilities at Onslow. Coming south, down the west coast of Australia, there were several useful little airfields at Learmouth, Caernavon, and Geraldton, but none possessed even the bare minimum of domestic accommodation or resources for technical work. In the time scale before the tests were due to begin, it would have been impossible to build much in the way of additional facilities, even if prefabrication techniques had been adopted. The scientific staff, responsible for analysing particulate samples from the radio-active clouds, had to be based alongside the air task group, and they, too, needed accommodation. Their laboratories were to be caravans, excellent vehicles, which could be moved by road, but the road to Onslow was not metalled and the prospect of driving vehicles towing caravans 800 miles from Fremantle to Onslow was not attractive.

Pearce Field, 750 miles south of Onslow and twenty miles east of Perth, was the only RAAF airfield in the whole region. It was an excellent, modern airfield, operating Vampire jet fighter-bombers, and had first-class accommodation. It was close to Perth and the port of Fremantle, where all the heavy equipment would be unloaded on arrival from the United Kingdom. On the other hand, it was a long way from Monte Bello and considerable additional airlift would obviously be required to satisfy all demands.

It was finally agreed to establish a main base at Pearce for all the aircraft, and to move some of them up to Onslow as required for each test. A transport shuttle service between Pearce and Onslow would be necessary during the build-up phase and when firing was in progress, but there did not appear to be any insuperable difficulties to mounting such a service. The airfields at Geraldton and Caernavon would make useful diversion airfields, if needed. Extra tarmac for aircraft parking and additional living accommodation for air and ground crews and scientific staff were considered essential and would have to be provided. The test series, to be known as Operation Mosaic, had April 1956 as the target date.

Detailed planning for Operations Buffalo and Mosaic were well in hand when early in August it was announced at one of the regular committee meetings that a third series of tests was to follow quickly after the Maralinga programme. This would include a megaton yield weapon and could not, of course, be mounted in Australia. A new test site had to be found, and a great deal of discussion centred around where. Some obvious possibilities were suggested, but just as quickly dismissed, because of the danger of fall-out whatever precautions might be taken. The experiences of the Americans at Bikini in 1954, when they exploded a very high yield weapon on a coral atoll and produced serious fall-out hazards over a vast area, were a solemn reminder of the dangers to be encountered in testing thermonuclear weapons. High yield weapons, if burst near the ground will produce fall-out problems wherever they are tested, but the Pacific Ocean seemed the only possible area in which to conduct the nuclear trials.

Mr (now Sir William) Cook, appointed Scientific Director for the series, attended the all-important meeting at which the difficult matter of selecting a site was discussed. Britain had claim to several islands in the Pacific that might be suitable, but the most obvious choice was Christmas Island, in what is known as the Line Group, about 1,000 miles south of Honolulu. It had been used by American forces during the war and, in addition to a lagoon from which flying boats had operated, had a small airstrip.

It was proposed, initially, that a naval survey party should reconnoitre the whole area; inspect Christmas, Malden, Penrhyn and other smaller islands and atolls, and report on harbours, anchorages, tides and general weather conditions for various times of the year. This, it was thought, would take seven to eight months and seemed to be a traditional, but very old-fashioned, method of getting what appeared to be relatively simple information. It was argued by the Air Ministry representatives that an expedition of this kind could be

69

completed in a matter of weeks if undertaken by air. A counter-proposal was that an aircraft, possibly a flying boat, would visit Christmas Island first, to see whether facilities built by the Americans still existed. If the runway was out of action, or a flying boat could not use the lagoon, complete photographic cover of the island and its existing facilities could still be obtained. If the aircraft could land, samples of rock and soil could be brought back, together with an assessment of repairs needed to rehabilitate the runway and any other facilities. It would be necessary to obtain the co-operation of the United States to stage through Honolulu and Canton Island, but this did not appear to present any difficulties.

By early September, the necessary operational instructions for the mission were issued to RAF Coastal Command, and on 16th September 1955, a force of three Shackletons, commanded by Wing Commander Tarrant left Ballykelly for Canton in the Phoenix Group of islands, by way of Goose Bay (Canada), Vancouver and Honolulu. They reached their destination on 22th September and immediately began their important photographic and survey tasks. The runway was in need of repair, but was still usable.

In addition to the normal aircraft crews, a major from the Royal Engineers and a lieutenant commander from the Navy flew with the party. It was their job to obtain as much information as possible on soil and rock structure, tides and weather at Christmas and Malden Island, assess the condition of the runway, harbour and beach landing facilities at Christmas Island, and record any other information considered useful for planning purposes.

All aircraft were fitted with RAF reconnaissance and survey cameras, supplemented by an assortment of private equipment. The party were working to a tight schedule and no time was lost in collecting the information. The most difficult, important and time-consuming operation was a photographic mosaic of the island; but this was completed without too much trouble, mainly because weather conditions were good. Excellent results were obtained with still and movie photography. Meanwhile, many items of information of interest and value to those engaged in planning the operation, were collected by expedition members.

The first aircraft arrived back in the United Kingdom on 15th

October and the second on 20th October. The third was delayed by engine trouble, but this was unimportant since all necessary information was brought back in the other two aircraft. It took about fourteen days to develop and print the films and produce mosaics of Christmas and Malden Islands. They were presented at the next meeting of the planning committee, just seven weeks after the problem had first been posed. There was unanimous agreement that Christmas Island would be entirely suitable as a main base for operations, and other islands would provide additional facilities for instrumentation.

To reduce physical damage and fall-out to a minimum, it was decided that all weapons should be exploded in the air, over the sea, and at an altitude that would prevent the fireball from coming into contact with the ground or the surface of the sea. Dropping the weapons from aircraft, or exploding them on balloons, were alternative methods of achieving the aim, but even though it had yet to be proved that dropping nuclear weapons from a Valiant bomber was feasible, scientific opinion was sufficiently confident in the RAF's ability to do this, that it was decided to plan on air drops as first choice for all the Pacific tests.

By November 1955 it was becoming abundantly clear that planning for all three operations was beyond the capacity of one small unit in the Air Ministry. Three planning teams were therefore established. The first, under Group Captain S.W.B. Menaul (who was also appointed Air Task Force Commander for the first two series at Monte Bello and Maralinga) was to plan the Mosaic tests at Monte Bello; the second under Air Commodore C.T. Weir was to complete planning for the Buffalo tests at Maralinga; and the third, under Air Vice-Marshal W.E. Oulton, was to plan the Pacific programme, to be known as Operation Grapple.

6

The Tests

Details of the first series of tests planned for May 1956, at Monte
Bello, became available at the end of October 1955. The primary
object of the trials was to test two nuclear weapons designed by the
Atomic Weapons Research Establishment at Aldermaston. No
secondary objectives, such as weapons effects on materials or
equipment, were specified.

The Task Force for the tests was a joint one. Scientists at
Aldermaston provided both the weapons and scientific teams to
explode them and analyse results; a detachment of Royal Engineers,
under Lieutenant-Colonel Holmes, built the steel towers on which the
weapons were exploded and prepared other important facilities on the
islands to meet the needs of the scientists. The Navy supplied a
variety of small ships, including HMS *Narvik*, an old tank-landing
ship, which provided excellent living and laboratory facilities for
scientists based on the islands. Commodore H.C. Martell was
appointed Commander of the Force.

The Air Task Group had to supply air and ground
communications, long range meteorological reconnaissance, shipping
safety patrols, photography, radiological surveys in the paths of the
radioactive clouds, ground survey of fall-out patterns and last, but
most important, radioactive samples of fission products from the
atomic clouds.

To meet these tasks it was estimated that a force consisting of a
squadron of Canberra jet bombers, a squadron of Varsity all-purpose
aircraft, Shackletons from Coastal Command for meteorological
work, helicopters, transport aircraft and long range maritime aircraft
for shipping patrols would be needed.

The Canberras had to be modified and fitted with special equipment for collecting samples from the radioactive clouds and for tracking the clouds at high level. Extra meteorological instruments had to be installed in the Shackletons, and a whole range of measuring and survey equipment for radioactive detection was added to the Varsities.

An old, deserted, wartime RAF Station at Weston Zoyland in Somerset was selected as an assembly point for the Air Task Group. No one seems to know why, but it could hardly have been more unsuitable, and during this period there was an extraordinary lack of interest in the whole project in certain RAF quarters, which became apparent later on, both in Australia and at Christmas Island.

The first Canberra of No76 Squadron arrived early in November and demonstrated in tangible form that a start had at last been made to form an Air Task Group. This was followed soon afterwards by the first Varsity, and by the end of the month Wing Commander R.C. Cobb arrived to supervise the initial build-up of the task force. Squadron Leader Boyd was appointed to take command of the Canberra Squadron and Squadron Leader Tew was to take charge of the Varsities. The Whirlwind helicopters were entrusted to Flight Lieutenant Verry and, after acceptance and testing, they were dismantled, crated and despatched by sea to Australia. Flight Lieutenant Verry and his crews followed in a charter aircraft.

The assembly of the force took nearly two months. They then had a comprehensive training programme to complete before setting out on the long flight to Australia. The entire Task Group was composed of volunteers, some of them national servicemen, who were determined not to miss a unique opportunity to take part in a very important venture, with an interesting Australia tour an added attraction.

From the moment Whitehall made the official announcement that a series of tests was to be carried out in Australia and on Christmas Island during 1956 and 1957, public interest sharpened. One reason was the knowledge, or belief, that Britain was at last on the threshold of producing her own nuclear weapons and becoming a nuclear power in her own right. Considerable Press interest had been apparent throughout the planning stages, but it reached a climax two days before the Task Force left for Australia, when more than fifty representatives from Press, Radio, Television and Film News Reels arrived at Weston Zoyland. They were given a full briefing on the scope of the tests and had an opportunity to talk to air and ground crews. Among the visitors were many well-known scientific and defence correspondents, some of whom later visited Maralinga to observe some of the tests.

The Air Task Group left for Australia on 15th March 1956 flying in easy stages by way of France, Egypt, Iraq, India, Malaya, Singapore, Darwin, along the north Australian coast to Broome and then to Pearce Field near Perth. The advance party had arrived a month before to prepare for the arrival of the aircraft and crews. It took another month to assemble equipment and establish communications at Onslow, position helicopters to provide transport to and from the Monte Bello Islands and complete a training schedule which had been devised for the Canberra sampling aircraft and the Varsities which were to carry out radiological surveys. Neptunes of the RAAF flew safety patrols.

Mr C.R. Adams from Aldermaston had been appointed Trials Director for the series and, after preliminary preparations involving collection and study of meteorological data, checks of the firing equipment and instrumentation on the islands, safety patrols, and a host of other tasks, the first test was planned for 4th May 1956. Unfortunately a cyclone, moving down the west coast of Australia from the general direction of the islands, caused a postponement until 16th May, but eventually the weapon was exploded successfully without incident. The Canberras penetrated the atomic cloud some six minutes after the explosion, to collect radioactive samples for the scientists based at Pearce Field. This was a more difficult task for the crews than similar duties at Nevada, where the crews were based at Indian Springs, only 35 miles from the Nevada site, whereas Pearce Field is 750 miles from Monte Bello.

The second test was completed satisfactorily on 19th June 1956, and at the beginning of July the entire task group moved from Pearce Field in Western Australia to Edinburgh Field in South Australia, in preparation for the second series of tests at Maralinga, planned for September. This series was to be more elaborate and demanding, since the test range was in the middle of the Australian continent, and therefore safety precautions had to be more strict. There were to be weapons effects tests associated with all the Buffalo trials to see how various items of equipment, such as tanks, aircraft, buildings, etc, stood up to the heat and blast effects from atomic explosions. There were also to be biological tests on animals, and from the RAF's point of view, the most important item of all, the first drop of an atomic bomb from a Valiant aircraft.

In all, four bombs were to be tested in the series, two on steel towers, one on the ground, and the air drop. The radioactive clouds from all four explosions would traverse half the Australian continent before drifting out to sea, so the safety precautions were more elaborate and demanded much greater effort from the Varsity survey and monitoring aircraft. Although the centre of the Australian continent is sparsely populated, it was necessary to follow the path of the cloud from each explosion, even when it was no longer possible to see it visually. The Australian Government appointed their own Safety Committee to monitor the tests and the trials director was responsible for seeing that agreed procedures were followed.

With the main elements of the Air Task Group established at Edinburgh Field, and the scientific and engineering groups in their aluminium village at Maralinga, all preparations for the first test were completed by the end of August. Sir William (later Lord) Penney, appointed Trials Director for the series, decided on 9th September for the first test. But bad weather intervened and, after a succession of postponements, the test, nicknamed "Penney's five o'clock rock", was completed on 27th September. Everything went according to plan; there were no incidents, and the Safety Committee expressed their satisfaction with the conduct of the test. The second test, a ground burst, was accomplished on time on 4th October. Although the air drop was originally planned as the grand finale, the Director decided to bring it forward as test number three. The Valiant crews had completed their training programme and on the afternoon of 10th October the weapon was loaded into the bomb-bay of Valiant WZ366, ready for take-off the following day, weather permitting.

Conditions continued to be favourable throughout the night, so in the morning the crew began the long list of preliminary checks to be made before the time set for take-off. Detonation was planned for 16.30 hours, but by midday the upper winds began to veer, and it was necessary to bring forward the whole schedule by one hour. This looked like the beginning of more delays and frustrations, but at 14.00 hours, when the crew were already in the aircraft, clearance was given for take-off.

The airfield was almost deserted except for a few ground crews and one or two scientists who had waited to see the aircraft off on its historic mission. It taxied to the end of the runway, completed final checks with a minimum of fuss, moved forward on to the runway and opened up to full power. This was the critical moment of the flight. At unstick speed she came gently off and began to climb away in a wide sweeping arc, clear of the range area. After reaching the allotted altitude, the crew began check runs over the dropping zone, to enable scientific staffs on the ground to adjust their equipment and make any last minute corrections. Everything appeared to be in order, and on receipt of final instructions from the controller the aircraft turned on to its heading for the dropping at 15.05 hours.

Very little was said in the cabin beyond what was necessary for the successful execution of the flight. The crew had a great responsibility and were determined to achieve as near perfection as possible in this all-important operation. All their attention was, therefore, devoted to the checks and counterchecks on equipment and procedures so necessary to ensure the best results.

A long run-in was made over flat desert, checking course, height, speed and other vital data continuously and cross-checking with radar monitoring equipment on the ground, right up to the release point. Not a word was spoken throughout this part of the flight and as the bomb aimer selected the red button on his release panel, he merely gave a thumbs-up sign to indicate that all equipment was functioning correctly. The final minute was the worst: the hopes of many people were pinned on this weapon, and ten years' development work was about to be put to the test. Finally in the last ten seconds, the count down followed by the calm voice of the bomb aimer reporting, "Bombs away".

There was a slight bump as the weapon left the aircraft, but otherwise nothing unusual. But immediately the bomb was released, the crew had to carry out a pre-planned manoeuvre to take the aircraft clear of the effects of the weapon at the instant of detonation, at the

77

same time counting-down the seconds for the time of fall, hoping that on the last one a blinding flash would signal a successful explosion. It did.

The crew then began their descent to the airfield by a much more direct route than that taken on the outward flight. They had time to reflect on the minutely planned procedures they might have had to put into operation if something had gone wrong. It somehow seemed an anticlimax that everything had worked so smoothly. After landing, the aircraft taxied to the concrete bay from which it had left only a short time before. Everyone was naturally elated at the success of the flight, but apart from a few words of thanks to the ground crew and scientists there was little to say or do. Britain's first drop of a nuclear weapon from an aircraft had been successfully accomplished at 15.30 hours, on 11th October 1956. It was an historic day and it seemed a pity that no one in authority from Whitehall or anywhere else in the United Kingdom, service or civilian, had been there to see it. It had taken a long time, but at last Britain had both the weapons and the means of delivering them. They were all British, entirely independent, and conferring on Britain the right to join the nuclear club as the third full member.

Many of those involved in Operation Buffalo had volunteered to move on to Christmas Island for the final series. The aircraft were in good condition and could be utilized; all, that is, except the Canberras which were still radioactive and too 'hot' to handle.

Christmas Island is the largest coral atoll in the Line Group of islands in the south-west Pacific, and was discovered by Captain James Cook in HMS *Resolution* on Christmas Day 1777. A small island at the entrance to the lagoon still bears his name and commemorates the event. The main island lies about 1,000 miles south of Honolulu, and 1,500 miles north-east of Fiji. It is approximately a hundred miles in perimeter, thirty-five miles long and twenty-four miles at its widest part. A reef several hundred yards in width surrounds the island, but to the west there is a substantial opening leading into a spacious lagoon. The island surface is almost uniformly flat, with only occasional sand dunes rising to between twenty and forty feet. Coconut palms are plentiful on the western side, but otherwise vegetation is confined to shrubs and tough prickly grass.

The climate is reasonably uniform; mean average temperatures are around 75°F and the maximum rarely exceeds 95°F. Even when high temperatures do occur, easterly trade-winds supply a cooling influence offsetting the effects of humidity giving a tolerable, even enjoyable, environment.

The entrance to the lagoon on the leeward side of the island provides a small harbour or safe anchorage, with a jetty and offloading facilities for shallow draught, ocean-going craft. Appropriately enough this little harbour is called Port London.

There are fairly detailed records of visits to Christmas Island, and short periods of occupation, over the past two hundred years since Captain Cook discovered it, but there are also indications that it was occupied even before that. Coconut palms were planted on the west side of the island by a British Company in 1902, and a London company carried on a copra business there until 1939. During the war, American forces used the island extensively and constructed an airstrip for the transit of aircraft of all kinds crossing the Pacific Ocean from the United States to battle areas in the war against Japan. They also dredged a channel to the north of Cook Island at the entrance to the lagoon, so that small tankers and supply ships could anchor or come alongside the jetty. Flying boats and floatplanes operated from the lagoon and after the war civil flying boats continued to use it.

The second island destined to play an important part in the Pacific tests was Malden, situated 400 miles south of Christmas Island. This is a flat, triangular-shaped coral atoll, about five miles long and four miles at its widest part. It was discovered by Captain Lord Byron in 1825 and, although there is little vegetation and even less water, wild pigs and wild cats, descendants of those left there during the last century, have managed to survive and breed healthy offspring. For many years, Malden was a rich and prosperous guano island, but it finally ceased operations in the late 'twenties, and was not occupied again until 1957, when a measurements group from the Grapple Task Force went ashore to install their instruments. Many relics of previous occupation were found, including a light railway with trucks still in working order.

There were no amenities on Christmas Island when the advance parties first set foot ashore, but they soon transformed it with all the paraphernalia which accompanies a scientific and military expedition of the size and complexity of the 1957 thermonuclear operations. Let it be said at once that the aim throughout their temporary occupation was to do as little damage as possible to the island and its people, and in this they succeeded. Rough dirt tracks almost completely circled the island, so it was possible to drive round the perimeter in a jeep. The landing strip, untouched since the war and in a poor state of repair, needed a great deal of reconstruction and extension before it could take Valiants, Canberras and other large aircraft in the traffic densities expected during the tests.

All weapons in this series were to be in the megaton range and could not, therefore, be detonated on or near inhabited territory, so a bombing area was selected at a point well out to sea off Malden, but using the island as an instrumentation base. The weapons were to be air-dropped and exploded at a height that would prevent the fireball touching the surface, thereby reducing fall-out hazards to a minimum, both in the dropping area and down-wind of ground zero. Two other islands, Penrhyn and Jarvis, were selected for siting meteorological stations and for instrumentation.

The effects of atomic and thermonuclear weapons are the same in principle, but the severity of each of the main phenomena varies with the yield of the weapon and can be calculated from relatively simple formulae. First, at the instant of detonation, is the flash, a short pulse of ultra-violet light many times brighter than the sun and capable of inflicting serious damage to vision if viewed directly even from fairly long range, depending on prevailing atmospheric and other conditions. Also at the instant of detonation is an immediate release of radiation, consisting of alpha, beta and gamma rays and neutrons. The greatest danger is from gamma and neutrons but their radius of effectiveness is confined to the area of burst, roughly the size of the fireball. Almost complete destruction of life and property takes place within this area anyway, so that the effects of immediate radiation are added to the terrible effects of the thermal pulse and the blast wave.

Millionths of a second after detonation the fireball begins to form and develops rapidly, reaching a maximum diameter of about two miles for a five-megaton bomb and six for a fifty-megaton one. If the burst is low and the fireball touches the ground, everything it encompasses will be vaporized. Accompanying the formation of the fireball is the second thermal pulse, which is infra-red and lasts for several seconds. Atmospheric phenomena can, of course, affect thermal radiation which travels in straight lines at the speed of light. Cloud, for example, can attenuate the heat if it is at or below the level of burst. High cloud above the point of burst, on the other hand, can act as a reflector and increase the intensity of heat over a particular area. Thermal radiation accounts for about one third of the energy released from a nuclear explosion and often produces the greatest damage from fire. Fabrics and dry materials may be ignited at distances up to twenty-five miles from the centre of a ten-megaton air-burst weapon, and fires may be caused over an even greater distance by progressive ignition of inflammable materials. Such conflagrations as have been started directly by the thermal pulse may be further aggravated by the destructive forces associated with the shock wave.

Immediately following the thermal pulse, the shock wave radiates outwards from the centre of the explosion at the speed of sound. Energy from most nuclear weapons in the form of blast accounts for just over half the total energy released. The effect of the shock wave from a ten-megaton air-burst weapon would be to destroy nearly everything within a radius of six miles, with progressively less damage at greater distances from the centre of the explosion. Associated with the movement of the shock wave are strong winds, often exceeding 200 mph, scattering small fires, starting new ones and fanning those already well alight. Blast damage varying from total destruction to repairable would extend out to a radius of about twenty miles for a 10-megaton air-burst weapon and about fifteen for a ground-burst one. Relatively this would cover most of the Greater London area and parts of the Home Counties; damage from the thermal pulse could then be expected to cover a distance equal to that from Southend to Farnham.

The remainder of the energy from a high yield thermonuclear weapon would be dissipated in the form of residual radiation from fall-out but, as already mentioned, this will be greatest in ground-bursts and will vary in extent according to the strength and direction of the prevailing wind. It could affect an area of up to ten thousand square miles whatever the conditions, if the fireball touches the ground.

Within this area all life would be seriously threatened and between ten and fifteen million casualties could result from just one such bomb burst over this country.

The United States 1954 tests at Bikini were carried out on atolls consisting mainly of coral. A whole island was vaporized by the force of one explosion of about five megatons, and since coral is mostly calcium carbonate, fall-out resulting from the mass of coral sucked up into the radioactive cloud was deposited over a wide area as radioactive dust in the form of unslaked lime. Prevailing winds were westerly, so an area to the east of the point of burst, elliptical in shape and extending to about 165 miles down-wind, was heavily contaminated. There was also a smaller area of contamination up-wind of the point of burst, extending to about twenty miles. At its widest point the ellipse was nearly forty miles across.

Estimates from data collected showed that radioactivity inside an area 140 miles long by twenty miles wide was sufficiently intense to have threatened the lives of all human beings who might have been living in the area. Radiation dosage from a nuclear explosion is measured in units called roentgens, and a dose of twenty-five roentgens received by a normal person over a brief space of time is enough to produce temporary changes in the blood though there is no lasting effect. A dose of 100 roentgens received over the same period of time would cause radiation sickness, and a dose of 450 roentgens over a period of twenty-four hours would probably be fatal to about half the number of people exposed to the source. A high radiation dose spread over a long period of time, on the other hand, produces much less effect.

The intensity of radiation near ground zero at Bikini was over 5,000 roentgens for the first thirty-six hours after fall-out began, and the highest radiation measured outside the atoll was 2,300 roentgens for the same period. This occurred on another atoll about a hundred miles away. Measurements of 1,000 roentgens were recorded 125 miles away. In all, an area of about 7,000 square miles down-wind of the explosion was so contaminated that the lives of any human beings who might have been living there would have been endangered.

If a weapon is exploded high in the air, either from a balloon or a missile, or dropped from an aircraft, so that the fireball does not touch the surface of the earth, radioactivity adheres only to the particles of the bomb casing or dust particles in the atmosphere, both of which will be extremely small and light. These tiny particles will be carried up into the stratosphere by the violence of the explosion and, being very light, will take a long time to descend. Strong upper winds will scatter them over a wide area and in some cases they might travel round the globe several times before finally falling back to earth. By this time the level of radioactivity will be only a fraction of what it was, most having been dissipated in the upper air. Radioactivity is at its most dangerous level during the first three or four hours after detonation, thereafter it decreases rapidly. In high air bursts, where no debris is sucked up into the radioactive cloud, hazards from fall out are infinitely less than from ground bursts.

Safety and security regulations adequate for atomic weapon explosions in the kiloton range would, of course, be totally unacceptable for those in the megaton range. Britain obviously could not have risked a repetition of the Bikini hazards in the Christmas Island tests, although in fairness to the Americans it must be acknowledged that valuable information resulting from their tests was made known to the world by the American Atomic Energy Authority. Without this information Britain's knowledge of the effects of thermo-nuclear weapons would have been far from complete. The Pacific tests were therefore planned from the beginning to be carried out at high level and consequently fall-out from them was negligible.

In common with the two previous tests in Australia, the Pacific tests were to be mounted by a joint task force from the three Services and the scientific establishment at Aldermaston. All the weapons were to be dropped from Valiants, sampling of the radioactive cloud was to be carried out by Canberras; the air lift, so essential to the success of all these tests, was to be provided by Hastings of RAF Transport Command, and meteorological tasks were allotted to Shackletons of Coastal Command. Other tasks such as communications between the islands were also the responsibility of the RAF.

The task force consisted of Navy, Army, RAF and Scientific Task Groups, each under a command from its own Service or Department. All groups were directly responsible to the task force commander for executing their allotted tasks. The Scientific Director was Mr (now Sir

William) Cook and his deputy was Mr Charles Adams, who had directed the Monte Bello tests in 1956. It was a formidable undertaking to weld such a large and diverse company into an efficient unit. Each element had its own traditional methods of doing things and some time-honoured prejudices and customs had to be overcome in the common interest. Air Vice-Marshal Oulton was the Task Force Commander.

Initially, the Army Task Group had the lion's share of the work in providing a host of facilities on Christmas Island before the other groups could begin to function. Apart from traces of American occupation during the war, Christmas Island was just another typical, tropical island with no natural resources except coconuts and fish. To mount operations on the scale of the 1957 tests required the construction of a small township, with a port, an airfield, road systems covering most of the island, main electricity, water (which had to be distilled from sea water), a sewerage system, fuel storage, living accommodation and food supplies. All the materials and equipment needed to meet these demands had to be brought from the United Kingdom, and this meant ships, operated by the Royal Navy and Merchant Navy, which brought essential supplies for basic construction and re-supply.

Reconstruction of the runway was a formidable task, involving clearing, excavating, compacting, levelling and surfacing a strip 7,000 feet long and 180 feet wide; concrete paving for aircraft standings and taxi tracks were also necessary. Airfield buildings included an air traffic control tower, operations centre and bulk storage for the enormous quantities of fuel needed for the jet and piston-engined aircraft soon to arrive on the island from the United Kingdom. Runways and a communications centre had to be provided at Malden and Penrhyn Islands, and to co-ordinate the activities of all three bases it was decided to establish a joint operations centre on the airfield at Christmas Island. Several specialist buildings for the storage and assembly of weapons were also required. Domestic accommodation for the whole force was to be provided by erecting tents, but more solid buildings were required for bulk food storage, bakeries, laundry and recreation facilities.

The first bridgehead on Christmas Island was established on 19th

June 1956, by the arrival of RFA *Fort Beauharnois* as a logistic support vessel and temporary headquarters for the advanced parties. She was followed on 24th June by the troopship HMT *Devonshire* bringing the Army, Navy and Air Force advanced contingents. The build-up of stores and equipment began the next day and gathered momentum in the months that followed, as a steady stream of vessels of all kinds arrived at the island, disgorged their cargoes and departed. By November, over 20,000 tons, including 600 vehicles — cranes, tractors, graders, bulldozers and many other types — had been landed at the little port of London. Some ships with large refrigerated storage capacity were used to store fresh rations; others provided distilled water until shore installations could be brought into action.

HMS *Warrior*, a light carrier, acted as operations control ship during live drops of weapons from the Valiants which took place off Malden Island some 400 miles south of Christmas Island, and the faithful old *Narvik*, which had given such valuable service at Monte Bello in the first series of tests, acted as a technical control and monitor ship. Two New Zealand frigates joined the task force as meteorological observation vessels, and a host of smaller craft played less spectacular, but very important, roles in the success of the operation.

The elaborate construction programmes on the islands were completed and facilities for operating all types of aircraft were available from the beginning of March 1957. Valiant crews, who were to drop the weapons, began their extensive training programmes in April, and the first test was completed successfully on 16th May 1957.

The second and most important of the four tests took place on 31st May. For this test, observers from the Commonwealth and the United States were flown out to Christmas Island, where they joined a large contingent of Press representatives from many parts of the world to watch the explosion. A large weapon in the megaton range, which the crews christened "The Penney Dreadful", was dropped from a Valiant bomber and burst with a flash that penetrated dark goggles on observers stationed nearly forty miles away. They felt the heat of the thermal pulse as from a furnace, when the giant fireball spread its doom-laden canopy over a vast circular area of ocean. The enormous mushroom cloud spiralled upwards into the stratosphere while condensation garlanded it with wispy rings of vapour. This was the most impressive thermonuclear explosion in the whole series and it did not disappoint the onlookers. No doubt, those who saw it will remember the terrible spectacle for the rest of their lives, and it did seem a pity that no British Members of Parliament, Senior or Junior Ministers, Chiefs of Staff, or even senior Military Commanders from the British Armed Services attended any of the nuclear tests carried out in 1956/57. Nearly every American President since the war, numerous Congressmen and most members of the Soviet Political and Military hierarchy have witnessed nuclear explosions. So, too, have senior French and Chinese political leaders and military commanders. As a result, public discussion of nuclear weapons in these countries, where it existed at all, was on the whole better informed than in Britain, and certainly less emotional.

It was six months before conditions were again suitable for testing, but in April 1958 another smaller task force was deployed - to Christmas Island and three more weapons were tested successfully. This completed Britain's thermonuclear weapons testing programme and, although it was not realized at the time, it was to be the end of all nuclear testing in Australia and at Christmas Island.

A new era for Britain and for the Royal Air Force had just begun. Britain had her own atomic and thermonuclear weapons whose proven efficiency and effectiveness equalled any in the world. The RAF had demonstrated its ability to operate in the nuclear role and British scientists had amassed a great deal of knowledge and experience in the field of nuclear physics; this was to prove of immense value to military and civil organizations in developing new techniques in nuclear science. Those who were lucky enough to have taken part in these historic events had a unique experience and a greater understanding of the importance of nuclear deterrence in maintaining world peace. They needed no convincing that Britain's possession of an independent nuclear deterrent force, during the decade in which Bomber Command provided that force, gave her greater authority in the councils of the world than she would otherwise have enjoyed, or enjoys today.

It took ten, long, hard years to produce a fully independent, credible and efficient nuclear force. It was costly in money and manpower, but it gave Britain all the technology and techniques required to become an independent nuclear power and to remain one. Costs of weapon systems have, of course, escalated in recent years and it would now be economically impossible for Britain to maintain a modern, credible, independent nuclear deterrent, even if it were vital to her survival to do so. But that does not mean that Britain should opt out of the nuclear field altogether as she may be forced to do unless steps are taken to keep abreast of technological developments in the nuclear aspects of war. Britain must also be prepared to revise her concept of nuclear strategy in the 1980s.

7

V-Bombers Operational

The years 1956-57 saw the most significant advances in the development of Britain's nuclear deterrent; indeed they might well be described as the climax of scientific and military endeavour that began ten years earlier. They were certainly momentous years for the officers and men who were privileged to serve in Bomber Command at that time. Many of them had seen the introduction into operational squadron service of the first of the V-bombers, the Valiant, and some had taken part in proof testing of atomic and thermonuclear weapons. Vulcans and Victors began to reach the squadrons towards the end of 1957, and throughout 1958 the build-up of squadrons and training establishments progressed satisfactorily.

The year 1957 was especially memorable for an event which at the time attracted a good deal of attention and interest, and generated considerable political and military controversy. This was the publication of Duncan Sandys' famous Defence White Paper. In a maze of other pronouncements on defence policy outlining new strategic concepts in the missile age, the Paper stated very simply that: "Britain must possess an appreciable element of nuclear deterrent power of her own".

But the Paper also made a more dramatic and revolutionary announcement. For some time, a group of government advisers had been harping on the theme that the missile would, in future, be the primary weapon in offensive and defensive air operations, so Defence Minister Sandys took the opportunity to announce in the White Paper that the primacy of the ballistic missile as a future strategic delivery vehicle had been established, and that it would replace manned aircraft in a few years. The United States at that time had, of course, already developed ballistic missiles, capable of delivering nuclear warheads over a range of 1,500 miles, with an accuracy sufficient to hit targets such as towns or industrial complexes with devastating results. Other, more effective, missiles capable of inter-continental ranges were under development. The British Government had decided to follow the example of the United States and, as a result of this dramatic change in defence policy, it was proposed that manned aircraft for the nuclear strategic role should not be developed beyond the V-bombers, which were just coming into squadron service. This decision was to have enormous repercussions in later years, but it did not retard production of the V-bombers or the programme for the creation of a British independent nuclear deterrent at that stage.

The 1957 White Paper set the pattern for British defence policy for at least a decade, during which the Royal Air Force moved ahead of the other Services in priority, and Bomber Command was accorded top priority, as the instrument of Britain's independent nuclear deterrent.

The Valiant training unit was well established at RAF Gaydon by the middle of 1956, and in 1957 the Vulcan operational conversion unit and the first two operational squadrons were formed at Waddington. The Vulcan training unit eventually moved to Finningley, where it remained throughout most of the life of the V-force. The first Victor squadron was formed at the end of 1957 and it was decided to place responsibility for training Victor crews on RAF Gaydon (already training crews for Valiants) as the commitment was somewhat smaller than the Vulcan task and Gaydon was large enough to cope with both requirements. This completed the general training pattern for the V-force and enabled those responsible for forming, equipping and training the new squadrons to get on with their jobs.

The Bombing School at Lindholme, in Yorkshire, where young aircrews were trained in the complex radar, navigation and bombing equipment they would have to use on joining an operational squadron in Bomber Command, was a very important link in the training organization. On completion of the course at Lindholme, crew members went to Gaydon or Waddington (later Finningley) where they joined captains and co-pilots for the remainder of their training as complete crews. Lindholme had been specially prepared and equipped to fulfil its important role in training the bomb aimers and navigators, and as the build-up of the V-force gathered momentum, it worked at very high intensity turning out the crews needed for newly formed squadrons. Although the course was already long and demanding, it was decided to add to it elementary instruction on nuclear weapons and their effects, so that navigators and bomb aimers, in addition to mastering the intricate equipment of their trade, would also have a good working knowledge of nuclear weapons. After all, they might one day have to drop them in anger.

As the Vulcan, Victor and Valiant squadrons expanded throughout 1958, Strategic Air Command (SAC) of the United States Air Force showed increasing interest in Bomber Command, its equipment and operational capability. Bomber Command had long admired the efficiency and strike capability of SAC and had maintained close and friendly relations which went back to when the 8th Air Force operated over Germany from UK bases. As the strength and operational efficiency of Bomber Command improved, the aircrews felt capable of challenging their more powerful partners, and in 1957 accepted an invitation from SAC to take part in one of their annual competitions, in which individual crews and units competed in navigation and bombing tests. Bomber Command sent a team to the United States for the first encounter, and thereafter similar confrontations at alternate venues were a regular feature in the training calendar.

In November 1957, the first exchange of ideas by experts on various aspects of strategic nuclear bombing techniques took place, when members of SAC visited Headquarters Bomber Command at High Wycombe to discuss joint operational planning, targeting and other problems of common interest, with the object of co-ordinating nuclear strike plans to their mutual advantage. From this developed a regular, free and full exchange of information on all matters relating to training, tactics and equipment for nuclear and conventional bombing. This happy and profitable arrangement continued until Bomber Command was abolished in 1968, and responsibility for Britain's strategic nuclear capability passed to the Royal Navy.

The close and friendly connections with SAC Headquarters were further strengthened in the latter part of 1957 by the establishment of direct communications links with 7th Air Division (a formation within SAC occupying airfields in Britain with Headquarters at High Wycombe on the other side of the hill from Bomber Command Headquarters). Telephone and teleprinter communications with 7th Air Division and with SAC Headquarters at Offutt Air Force Base, near Omaha, Nebraska, were installed in Bomber Command operations centre, but the telephones were neither red nor blue, nor were they for the purpose of taking orders from SAC as some ill-informed detractors in political and Press circles were fond of proclaiming prior to the 1964 General Election. From 1957 onwards, visits by officers from HQ Bomber Command to SAC became more frequent. Bomber Command regularly sent teams to Omaha, and they returned the compliment by coming to High Wycombe. The Commander-in-Chief usually paid one or two visits a year to America, including a call on the Commander, Strategic Air Command, who was no stranger to Bomber Command. These exchanges had always been regarded as natural, important and extremely beneficial to both sides. Another feature of those early days was the flow of distinguished visitors to Bomber Command from organizations at home and abroad, to hear and see something of the Command's capability and how it operated. They kept the stations busy demonstrating that the British taxpayer's money was being spent wisely, and the equipment it purchased used efficiently.

The most significant aspect of the 1958 Defence White Paper (Cmnd 363), from Bomber Command's point of view, was the statement: "If the deterrent influence of the bomber force is to be effective, it must not be thought capable of being knocked out on the ground". Simple and, perhaps, glaringly obvious as this may appear, it nevertheless gave authority for Bomber Command to develop an elaborate dispersal system for the whole bomber force. This involved not only additional airfields to which aircraft could be flown in times of tension or emergency, but a complex communications system to control the force when it was dispersed and get it off the ground quickly when danger threatened. This exceptional dispersal scheme will be dealt with in a later chapter when the significance of it will be seen against the threat to this country, particularly from Soviet Intermediate Range Ballistic Missiles (IRBM) which were deployed in

Western districts of the Soviet Union in increasing numbers from 1960 onwards.

The expansion of Bomber Command with all three types of V-bombers was progressing satisfactorily, if not spectacularly, in 1958 when a new, powerful and very different type of weapon system, forecast in the 1957 Defence White Paper, was added to the striking power of the Command. This was the American IRBM, Thor, which entered squadron service as a complementary system to the V-bomber force, but with control of the nuclear warheads for the missile exercised by United States Air Force personnel under what was called "the double key" system. In the same year, the McMahon Act was amended to allow limited exchanges of information between the United States and friendly powers on the design and production of nuclear weapons. Britain was the first and only country to benefit from this modification to American policy.

It was not fully appreciated at that time how much ballistic missiles, and particularly inter-continental missiles then reaching the testing stage, would change the whole concept of nuclear deterrent philosophy. Since there was no immediate prospect of any form of defence against ballistic missiles once they were launched, the menace of a pre-emptive attack became more real, and this demanded new safeguards for the deterrent strike forces which, in turn, ushered in the "counter-force strategy", which dominated strategic thinking in the early 'sixties. The advent of Thor, therefore, not only introduced a new weapons system, it heralded the arrival of the ballistic missile as the primary instrument of strategic nuclear deterrence. Today, new and more powerful missile systems, launched from hardened ground silos or submarines, are deployed in the nuclear deterrent role by all the major nuclear nations and as yet there is no absolute defence against them, even if the anti-ballistic missile treaty had not been signed in 1972. Ballistic missiles as vehicles for strategic bombardment were, of course, born as the result of research and development by German scientists and engineers at the famous Peenemunde establishment on the Baltic coast in the closing years of the last war, and were used operationally, albeit in primitive form, against targets in Britain in August 1944. They came too late to influence the course of the war in Europe, and had it not been for the overwhelming power of Bomber

Command, which destroyed the launch sites with clinical precision, an enormous amount of damage would have been inflicted on London and adjacent areas.

It will be remembered that preoccupation with the defence of the Fatherland against the mounting allied bombing offensive from 1942 onwards forced Germany progressively on to the defensive, until the fatal state was reached of putting practically all aircraft productive capacity on to building fighters, in a vain and desperate attempt to stem the bomber onslaught. Their final solution to the problem of how to resume some form of offensive air war against Britain was both progressive and militarily sound. The weapons launched against this country in 1944 were technically ahead of anything under development in Britain or America. First came the V1 "flying bombs", which had a short, effective life and an inglorious end, but they gave our defences a great deal of trouble while the assault lasted. Next, and by far the most menacing, was the appearance of the V2 rocket missiles.

The V2 attacks could be described as a continuation of Germany's long-range artillery bombardment of Channel coast targets and shipping, but with improved range to enable attacks to be made on targets well inland. From launch sites in northern France and the Low Countries, these rockets could reach London. There was no possible defence against them except by air attack on the launch and storage sites; they could not be intercepted in the air, nor could warning of their approach be given. Fortunately, their reign of terror was short-lived, and the majority of launch and storage sites had been neutralized by bombing when the Normandy landings took place. During their short operational life, the V2s created a great deal of concern, took their toll of life and damage to property, and heralded a new era in strategic bombardment; yet one which was extraordinarily slow to develop in the post-war years. Soon after the war ended, many of Germany's best scientists were available either in Western Europe or America with a wealth of knowledge and experience of this kind of warfare, but it was more than ten years before a strategic nuclear weapons system, based on the rocket missile principle, appeared on the military scene.

The main reasons for lack of progress in ballistic missile design in the immediate post-war years were the difficulties in finding a suitable fuel (which, in turn, determined engine design and performance for the ranges required) and guidance systems with sufficient accuracy over long distances. By 1954, improved techniques, manufacturing processes and new fuels were available to make missiles a practical proposition for short-range operations. Considerable research and development into guidance systems had also been carried out, particularly in the United States, and when an effective missile system finally emerged, some people in positions of authority in this country erroneously assumed that aircraft in the strategic strike role were obsolete and would be replaced entirely by missiles within a few years. But it did not work out quite as simply as the self-appointed experts had foretold. Even when the first missiles had been produced with sufficient range to reach important targets in the Soviet Union, and were able to carry nuclear warheads, there remained problems of accuracy, reliability, deployment and security, the solutions to which were to prove both expensive and time consuming.

British defence policy at that time envisaged the main function of the ballistic missile as a nuclear deterrent force, providing a means of retaliation, or the threat of retaliation, against nuclear attack in exactly the same way as manned aircraft had done since the nuclear deterrent philosophy of massive retaliation was first adopted. A missile force, like any other strike force, will be successful and achieve its aim until an enemy believes he can reduce its capacity to retaliate by pre-emptive strike, to the extent that any risk of damage to his own forces, industrial complexes or cities would be negligible, or at worst acceptable. In planning his offensive an enemy must take account of the number and vulnerability of the missiles he believes to be ranged against him, and it is reasonable to assume that he will be able to calculate within acceptable limits the strength of the retaliatory force.

The deterrent value or credibility of a missile force can be measured in terms of its strike capability, its speed of reaction and its ability to survive pre-emptive attack. Thus, deployment, security and control are of primary importance in the operation of a ballistic missile force, just as they were, and are, in operating a manned bomber force. Missiles are normally launched from platforms, whether operated from land bases, aircraft, or ships on or under the sea, so deployment poses problems not previously encountered in other weapons systems. Britain was the first country in the world to face these problems in a practical way, when she took delivery of United States Thor missiles in 1958. The Thor force was certainly the first operational missile system in the West, and, as far as was known, in the world, and Britain was the first country to operate a strategic nuclear force of ballistic missiles and manned aircraft, fully integrated in one Command structure.

The story of Thor goes back to December 1955, when the United States Government awarded the Douglas Aircraft Company of Los Angeles a research and development contract for an intermediate range ballistic missile, with the code name Thor. A number of sub-contractors were responsible for propulsion, guidance and the re-entry vehicle. Within ten months of the development contract being signed, Thor was delivered to Cape Canaveral (now Cape Kennedy) for trials, and the first one was launched three months later, 25th January 1957. The first four launches were failures, but the fifth was successful, and in less than twenty months a major new weapons system had been designed, developed, produced and successfully launched — a truly remarkable achievement. But Thor had one serious limitation, its range was just 1,500 miles and it could not, therefore, reach targets in the Soviet Union from launch bases in America.

In March 1957, the British Prime Minister, Harold Macmillan, and the President of the United States, Dwight D. Eisenhower, met in Bermuda. Among military subjects discussed was the possibility of deploying Thor in the United Kingdom and, not surprisingly, the outcome was an agreement to deploy sixty Thor missiles in Britain manned by the Royal Air Force (Bomber Command), but control of the nuclear warheads was to be the responsibility of the United States through US Air Force personnel attached to each Thor unit. This latter condition complied with United States law regarding custody of nuclear weapons and dissemination of nuclear knowledge, but it did not hinder the efficient operation of the missile force.

A Government to Government agreement was signed on 22nd February 1958 by Sir Harold (later Baron) Caccia, British Ambassador in Washington, on behalf of the United Kingdom, and by Mr Christian Herter, United States Secretary of State. This was

Another thermonuclear cloud. Christmas Island 1957.

A Canberra climbing to enter the thermonuclear cloud for particle samples, Christmas Island 1957.

Crews of the Valiants involved in the dropping of Britain's first nuclear bomb.

Valiant bombers of the Royal Air Force.

An unsuccessful contender for the V-bomber series, the Short SA-4 Sperrin which reached the prototype stage.

The delta-winged Vulcan B2 carrying a Blue Steel stand-off missile under its fuselage.

A Blue Steel stand-off missile being unloaded from its special transporter vehicle to a loading trolley for mounting on a Victor.

The crescent-winged Victor B2 carrying Blue Steel under the fuselage.

Victor B1A in a conventional role dropping 35 × 1000-lb bombs.

A Thor missile of the RAF on its launch pad.

followed by a technical agreement between Royal Air Force and United States Air Force representatives which, among other things, provided for the setting up of a joint RAF/USAF committee to resolve problems arising out of the decision to deploy Thor in the United Kingdom. Planning was complicated by the need for speedy action, as it had been confirmed in 1957 that Russia was also developing an intermediate range ballistic missile capable of attacking targets in this country and in Europe; Thor was required to maintain the West's lead in nuclear strike capability.

Normally in joint USAF/RAF projects it might be expected that, as a first step, outline plans within strict financial limitations would be approved and each successive stage scrutinized at financial planning levels; but such was the urgency of the Thor project that conventional practices were ignored, or greatly modified, and economy for once was subservient to speed in planning and production. One of the most important benefits in planning the Thor programme was the availability of a large number of disused airfields in East Anglia, Lincolnshire, Yorkshire and the Midlands, but even though there were plenty of possible deployment bases to choose from, they did not all have the necessary features required for missile sites.

The force was to consist of four main bases each with four satellites with a clutch of three missiles. No clutch of weapons was to be sited nearer than ten miles from another, giving a good dispersal pattern to present a considerable targeting problem to a potential enemy. The four main bases selected were the RAF Stations at Feltwell, Hemswell, Driffield and North Luffenham, and their satellites were spread from Yorkshire southwards to Norfolk. In planning the design and construction of the weapon sites, normal contractual procedures had to be modified to enable design and engineering work to be completed in the shortest possible time, and while there were many advantages to be gained by locating the sites on existing airfields, whether active of inactive, it was still necessary for special teams of engineers and surveyors to cover the whole of eastern and central England before the twenty most suitable airfields could be selected.

Construction began at Feltwell in August 1958. As this airfield was close to the USAF base at Lakenheath, it was possible to fly in many items of equipment direct from the United States and this practice was

97

later adopted for the other main bases. As might be expected in a venture of this kind, many new problems were uncovered during construction work, not least the conversion from United States engineering practices to British. For example, all electrical components were designed for American voltage and had to be converted to British equivalents. The reception, inspection and maintenance building on each main base was a converted aircraft hangar, and these had to be equipped with special control units for air conditioning and temperature control to US specifications; but the units were designed in the United Kingdom and manufactured by British sub-contractors. Full advantage was taken of the experience gained in designing and planning the first site for application to others, enabling all twenty to be completed in just under twenty-five months from the date of the installation committee's first meeting. During the installation phase, the USAF Military Air Transport Service lifted about 80% of the entire weapons system and initial spares support direct from Southern California to the airheads at, or near, the operational airfields in Britain. The build-up was rapid. In February 1959, sixty-three aircraft delivered hundreds of tons of equipment to Hemswell, and in July, seventy-six flights were made to Driffield. Complete Thor missiles were air transported in giant freight aircraft, thus saving time and space, particularly in packing, unpacking and reassembly.

This was one of the most successful, co-ordinated efforts covering building, civil engineering, electrical and mechanical installation, ever achieved in missile deployment, or for that matter in any weapons system, and was an object lesson on how military contracts can be completed on time and according to plan when the will to meet contractual agreements is present and the urgency of the project demands, and gets, high priority. Thor was developed under the then comparatively new concept called "concurrency", a concept which required parallel action during the development phase of a weapon for its production, deployment and the training of its support and operating personnel.

The programme overall was managed by a single USAF Programme Director, vested with complete responsibility for policy, funding, testing and development in the field; the RAF was represented by a team of officers located within the office of the Programme Director. The aim was to produce an operational system in the shortest possible time. To achieve this a policy of freezing designs at an early stage was adopted, while development was planned to continue during operational deployment. By using existing individual systems and components of known and proven design to the maximum extent, the Thor weapons system was fully operational in the United Kingdom just four and a half years after signing the original design contract. By adhering to a policy of progressive development in the field, in which information was fed back to the design and development teams at the manufacturers, many improvements were incorporated in the missiles, resulting in superior operational performance and improved reliability. In the latter part of the life of Thor, for example, the count-down was reduced by nearly half.

When the major build-up of equipment was completed in 1959, Thor airheads were closed down and re-supply requirements flown in to selected RAF and USAF stations. From May 1960, this arrangement was confined to major items and normal spares re-supply was by civil airline to London Airport and thence by road to Thor stations. Repairable items of equipment were returned to contractors in the United States by the same routes, and this comprehensive logistic system enabled high priority demands to be satisfied in about fifty hours over a distance of 6,000 miles – an achievement not possible with ordinary support from our own manufacturers in this country, mainly because of the complicated system we had to adopt to obtain spares.

Initially, all training for the Thor force was carried out in the United States, first at Davis-Monthan Air Force Base, near Tucson, Arizona, and later at Vandenberg in California which, in addition to training facilities, is the head of the Pacific missile range and Headquarters of the 1st Missile Division of the USAF. Some 250 officers and 1,500 airmen of the RAF were trained between June 1958 and February 1960; during this period they launched nine Thor missiles, seven of which were successful. When deployment started in the United Kingdom, the United States Air Force provided a field training detachment at Feltwell to assist in establishing and maintaining the first squadron. Subsequently, selected personnel from this squadron visited other main bases to help form the maintenance wings of new units. When the force was fully established, all training was concentrated at a new Strategic Missile School based at Feltwell and run by Bomber Command.

The first Thor had arrived at Feltwell on 19th September 1958 from Lakenheath, the airhead for missiles and equipment flown in from America. Other Thors quickly followed to Hemswell and Driffield, and with the last base, North Luffenham, completed a force of sixty missiles joined an already formidable manned aircraft force of more than 180 V-bombers, all armed with megaton weapons operated by Bomber Command. Every three months during the lifetime of the missile force, one Thor was flown back to America from its base in Britain for test firing. For the crews selected to accompany it, this was a reward for good service and an encouragement to further effort in the constant search for operational improvements. After passage from England to Vandenberg, the missile was put on a test and operational training programme lasting six weeks, culminating in a live firing of a missile down the Pacific range. These detachments were always very popular with Thor crews and the launching of a live missile was proof of the effectiveness of drills and procedures practised on operational deployment. This gave a convincing demonstration of weapon reliability and crew proficiency in the art of ballistic missile deterrence and missile warfare – one aspect of which was to be tested under realistic conditions during the Cuban missile crisis of 1962.

Thor was criticized as a retaliatory, or second strike, weapon on the grounds that it was "soft skinned", and could be destroyed in a surprise attack by opposing missiles or aircraft. In 1959, this statement was partially true but ignored the situation prevailing at the time when Thor was deployed in Bomber Command and for some considerable time afterwards. There was, in fact, no opposing missile force capable of destroying Thor in 1959. Even when the Russian intermediate range missile force was deployed in sufficient strength to threaten Thor, the destruction of small, dispersed targets such as missile sites was shown to be much more difficult than had been supposed. Considerably more than one missile with a megaton warhead would have been needed to be sure of knocking out each site, and increasing the yield of the warheads in the attacking missiles would not entirely have compensated for inaccuracies in delivery (or in-flight failures of the weapons) since blast damage from nuclear explosions increases only as the cube root of the yield.

Thus, when the Thor force became operational in 1958, and for at least two years afterwards, Russia did not have either the number or quality of missiles to destroy it. The main Soviet strategic strike force was the Air Force, equipped with Tu-95 (Bear), Tu-16 (Badger) and Mya-4 (Bison) aircraft, and a surprise attack with these delivery systems was simply not possible. Thor remained a valid deterrent force for most of its operational life, but by 1963 the situation had changed. Russia had considerably increased her missile force, although the advantage which she appeared to gain by so doing was already offset by America's deployment of an intercontinental strategic missile force consisting initially of Atlas and Titan missiles, and later Minuteman, and by the construction of a ballistic missile early warning system, operated from Alaska and Greenland, giving cover and warning of missiles launched against North America from bases in Russia. Thor was only an interim system designed to last about four years, and when this span of life came to an end there was no reprieve, even though many improvements had been incorporated in the missiles during operational deployment, notably in count-down time. Nor was Thor replaced by any other missile system despite the advantages – which Bomber Command had demonstrated – of operating a combination of manned aircraft and ballistic missiles; a concept recognized by all nuclear powers during the 'sixties as the ideal. America adopted this strategy with a wide range of weapons systems, familiarly known as the mixed force concept. Russia and France followed suit, and only Britain opted out. But missiles above ground were no longer credible in 1963, since they could in theory be destroyed by nuclear attack with similar missiles, and protection became imperative if they were to continue to pose a credible deterrent.

The V-bombers and Thor both carried megaton warheads. The speed of reaction of the bombers to attack from any source ensured their credibility as a nuclear retaliatory force and therefore as a deterrent. Thor missiles in the early part of their deployment could be

101

held at twenty minutes readiness for long periods, which was ample against the main threat at that time, namely, the manned bomber. But if they were to continue to be effective in the face of a missile threat it became clear that they would have to be put underground in hardened silos for protection; a difficult and expensive operation, as we learned from the Americans, who had embarked on just such a scheme for solid-fuelled Minuteman missiles. Thor was, therefore, honourably retired from its bases in Britain and flown back to the United States. But its retirement was short-lived. Such was its reputation for reliability and accuracy, ease of maintenance and mobility that it soon became an important item in America's space inventory and many of the original weapons have since played an important role in American space launches.

Much has been written and spoken over the years about the superiority of ballistic missiles over manned aircraft in the nuclear deterrent role. In the mid-'fifties, missiles captured the imagination of politicians and amateur strategists, but were more cautiously accepted by professionals as an introduction to a new era in strategic bombardment. The Royal Air Force and the United States Air Force shared the view that missiles could, eventually, replace aircraft in the strategic nuclear role, but the change-over would be gradual and not necessarily total. Nevertheless, ballistic missiles in the nuclear deterrent role were an accomplished fact even in 1958, and the 1959 Defence White Paper was quite specific on the question of future weapons systems. The missile was given pride of place among new weapons systems for both offensive and defensive forces. Up to this time, the RAF had been pursuing normal planning policy and looking ahead to the new generation of aircraft that would replace the V-bombers. An 8-turbojet supersonic bomber, the Avro 730, was already in the design stage. So, too, was an advanced, variable-geometry design which was receiving Government financial support. Both were cancelled in favour of a ballistic missile to be known as Blue Streak.

Blue Streak in 1957 was Britain's first and only venture into the strategic ballistic missile field. Its original design specified a liquid-fuelled missile using kerosene and liquid oxygen to power its two Rolls-Royce engines and develop about 280,000 pounds thrust.

This gave the missile a range of 2,500 miles and fully met the Air Staff's requirement for a missile capable of attacking targets in Russia from home bases. As mentioned earlier, the credibility of a deterrent force is measured by whether or not it can be destroyed, or drastically reduced in effectiveness, by pre-emptive attack, and, if not, how effective it would be in retaliation, having survived an initial enemy attack with nuclear weapons. The enemy must assess two factors: first, the effort needed to reduce the effectiveness of the deterrent force to a degree which would render it incapable of efficient retaliation and secondly, whether the effort needed to achieve this aim would be worth the cost, assuming it to be achievable. Blue Streak could have been operated from underground silos capable of withstanding very heavy overpressures from high yield nuclear weapons. Its reaction time was designed to be not more than ten minutes, and might possibly have been as little as two. A plan to disperse the missiles singly, each in its own hardened silo, would have presented an enemy with a difficult targeting problem. Not only would each site have required a heavy weight of attack to neutralize it, but there would have been a large number of sites, widely distributed and carefully concealed.

The concept of Blue Streak as originally proposed by its designers was very much in line with the practices adopted in America and Russia. But the cost would have been enormous and British experience with Thor had clearly indicated that liquid-fuelled missiles had serious limitations. The most effective land-based ballistic missile systems in the era of counter-force strategy were undoubtedly solid-fuel missiles, in hardened silos, with a very high reliability factor and almost instantaneous reaction. Blue Streak, as a liquid-fuelled missile, would not have met these requirements by the time it was due in service and many expensive modifications would have been necessary to bring it up to changing operational standards. It was therefore cancelled as a vehicle for strategic strikes in 1960.

This, as it turned out at the time, was not an irreparable loss to the Royal Air Force. It was still in the ballistic missile business with the prospect of obtaining the American air-launched ballistic missile, Skybolt, due to come into service in 1964. Nevertheless, something like £80 million had already been spent on Blue Streak with no possibility of it entering service in an operational role, so some return for this vast capital outlay was clearly desirable. It did, eventually, find employment as the basis of a joint European space project called ELDO, in which France and Britain agreed to promote a co-operative programme of space research, aimed at launching a satellite into orbit. Without Blue Streak there would not have been a suitable launch vehicle available in Europe. By 1962, Britain, France, West Germany, Holland, Italy, Belgium and Australia had combined to finance the launching of a satellite called *Europa*, and Blue Streak was to provide the main booster for the project. Alas, by 1968, this project, like so many others, had wilted and died through lack of financial support — particularly by Britain.

A ballistic missile in any form has advantages and disadvantages, whether it is launched from silos on land, from submarines in the depths of the ocean or from manned aircraft in the limitless wastes of the upper atmosphere. One common characteristic of ballistic missiles in 1960, appertaining even today, was relatively high invulnerability after launch. Among advantages that may be claimed for most missiles are speed, range, fast reaction and invulnerability (in silos, submarines or on aircraft in the stratosphere). Missiles can carry high yield nuclear warheads whose accuracy has been greatly improved (though against small precision targets they still do not match manned aircraft in this respect); they can carry their own counter-measures and decoys and can be kept abreast of defence system developments.

The main disadvantages are that once launched, missiles cannot be recalled though they may be made inert. Ground or sea-launched missiles are inflexible, in that they cannot be switched to alternative targets after launch, and while employed in the nuclear deterrent role they cannot be used for conventional purposes. The concept of the air-launched missile, on the other hand, offered a weapons system less susceptible to attack on the ground because wide dispersal could be adopted for both missiles and aircraft, thereby obviating the need for expensive underground silos. Missiles mounted on aircraft also appeared to offer greater mobility and flexibility than ground-launched or Polaris missiles in submarines, so that in combination with free-fall nuclear or conventional weapons mounted in the same aircraft a variety of tactics was possible. For example, air-launched missiles

104

could have been used to blast a way through enemy defences, enabling the aircraft with free-fall nuclear bombs to follow up and attack a selection of targets including those requiring precision bombing or those not previously identified. Manned aircraft were also capable of being recalled right up to the moment of missile launching or penetration of enemy airspace and, looking ahead to the future, manned aircraft seemed to offer the only sure means of attacking anti-missile defences if they ever appeared as a practical means of limiting ballistic missile attack. Both Bomber Command and Strategic Air Command were convinced that an air-launched ballistic missile was a logical and desirable step in the development of strategic nuclear forces.

8

Soviet Missile Threat

Britain's nuclear deterrent and nuclear strike capability in 1959 was certainly formidable, but the Air Ministry and Bomber Command were fully alive to the fact that the liquid-fuelled Thor missiles on fixed bases above ground would become vulnerable to enemy missile attack if and when an intermediate range ballistic missile force was deployed against Europe. The V-bombers, armed with free-falling bombs, required deep penetration of enemy territory to reach many of the important targets on the strategic target list. The deployment of surface-to-air missiles in defensive systems, the greatly improved margin in performance which technology was giving to modern jet fighters, improvements in Russian early warning radar control and reporting systems, and the interception capability of their new generation of interceptor fighters, had clear implications. In a few years' time, deep penetration of a highly developed air defence system would be difficult and costly, even at the heights and speeds at which the V-bombers could fly. The shooting down of an American U-2 reconnaissance aircraft, piloted by Gary Powers in 1960, by Soviet surface-to-air missiles confirmed what had been foreseen at least a year earlier.

It had been appreciated even before 1959 that the problems created by continuing improvements in Russian defences would almost certainly prove to be insurmountable, using normal high-level attacks by aircraft with free-falling bombs employing simple evasive tactics and electronic countermeasures. Developments in tactics and equipment are a continuous process in any military organization, but particularly in strategic air forces. Those concerned with the complicated business of maintaining credible nuclear deterrents attempt to forecast, as accurately as possible, likely improvements in enemy defence systems at any particular time and then take steps in advance to counter them, within the financial and other limitations prevailing at the time. It is by no means easy to forecast exactly what new tactics or equipment an enemy might adopt, and all too often the forecasts are not confirmed.

As early as 1954, the Air Staff, in conjunction with the scientific staffs, had considered the possibility of a powered bomb which could be carried part of the way to the target by a V-bomber, released to continue its journey under its own power and guidance, and deliver a nuclear warhead to a selected target without assistance from external sources or interference from enemy defences. The aircraft would be able to turn away immediately after release of the missile before reaching hostile airspace, guarded by surface-to-air point defences which, it was foreseen, would be the next logical step in the development of Russia's defence system.

In 1954, therefore, the Air Ministry Operational Requirements Directorate issued details for such a weapon suitable for carriage on Vulcans and Victors, to be produced by industry within four years. This weapon was code-named Blue Steel, and it was expected that an improved version could follow up to counter later improvements in enemy defences. It will be recalled how the application of strategic air bombardment developed from hit and miss techniques in 1914, when bombs were thrown over the side of the aircraft with a curse or a prayer and no more accurate means of guiding them than an inspired guess. Crude bombsights, referred to by later generations as bent wire aiming devices, designed in the 1920s and improved in the 1930s, were eventually superseded by the highly efficient, stabilized, automatic bombsights of World War II. Finally, radar navigation and bombing equipments, invented by British scientists in the last three years of the war and perfected for fitting to V-bombers, brought the art of high level strategic bombing to a degree of proficiency that appeared to leave little room for further development, though bombing errors were still relatively large by today's standards.

Throughout the years when these advances were being made, aircraft were flying higher and faster until the "forward throw" of a free-falling bomb from the latest marks of V-bombers exceeded ten miles, depending on the height and speed at which the aircraft was flying at the moment of release. This in effect gave the bomber "stand-off" capability, but the deployment of surface-to-air missiles, first in a point defence system which later spread to area defence, demanded new weapons and new tactics, if the requirement to put a bomb close to the aiming point was to be assured in the face of improved and enlarged enemy defences employing modern jet fighters and surface-to-air-missiles. Powered bombs offered a solution and Blue Steel was designed and produced in an attempt to restore the balance in favour of the strike aircraft — the V-bombers. In concept at that time it was probably one of the most advanced weapons anywhere in the world.

Blue Steel was a large weapon, carrying a megaton warhead, streamlined like a bomb with a rear-mounted delta wing and small delta foreplanes for pitch control. In-board ailerons on the wings and a pair of stabilizing fins, the lower one of which folded sideways to give ground clearance when attached to the aircraft, completed the control surfaces. The missile was in effect a small aeroplane, weighing about the same as a Meteor fighter, and was, if anything, more complicated. It was driven by a rocket engine using liquid propellants which gave it a speed several times that of sound at very high altitudes. It had its own inertial navigation system, automatic pilot and flight computer. It carried its own electric power for heating and operating servo-mechanisms to enable changes in course to be transmitted from the flight computer to the auto-pilot and thence to the control surfaces.

The operating technique was relatively simple. Each aircraft carried its missile to high altitude on the way to the target. Whilst in flight, the navigation systems of the aircraft and the missile were integrated, so that accurate calculations of position made by the aircraft's crew were continuously fed into the missile. Immediately on release from the aircraft, the missile fell away under gravity for a few seconds until the rocket engine ignited; it then began its programmed climb, accelerating rapidly as the rocket motor developed full power. Once on its programmed trajectory, the missile was on its own and needed no further assistance from its parent aircraft, which was free to turn away and return to base. The missile's inertial navigation system computed changes of velocity from ultra-sensitive acceleration measurements, calculated its position and compared it with the position of the target it had to reach, made any necessary changes in course through its flight computer, auto-pilot and control surfaces, thereby steering to its target. Directional control was on the twist and steer principle, in which each turn was begun by rolling with the ailerons and maintained by increasing lift on the foreplanes.

At high supersonic speeds, Blue Steel could not be intercepted by any existing defence system. It did not depend on signals or radar information from outside sources, and its navigation system could not be jammed. Its range, initially, was sufficient to enable the aircraft to stand well outside the surface-to-air missile defences then being developed in the Soviet Union, but it was realized that it would not enjoy immunity indefinitely – few weapons systems to date have achieved that unique characteristic. An improved version was therefore designed for introduction into Bomber Command about two years after the original design, but all work on the new project was cancelled when agreement was reached with the United States for the purchase of Skybolt. Blue Steel was an interim weapon, leading logically to the air-launched ballistic missile, and filled the gap admirably in the high level role in the interim period. No one could have foreseen at that time that decisions to be taken two years later would compel Bomber Command to revise its whole operational concept in which Blue Steel was to continue to give sterling service but using very different tactics.

Strategic Air Command in the United States faced similar problems to those confronting Bomber Command in maintaining a credible deterrent, and developments took a similar course. But American scientists were thinking further ahead to a weapon with sufficient stand-off range to enable the launch aircraft to remain outside enemy defences altogether – even including early warning radar – and fire a weapon on an accurate trajectory to a selected target deep into enemy territory. This was a logical and sensible proposal, which would have provided a counter to any likely developments in defence systems for at least a decade. Such a weapon was an obvious replacement for Blue Steel, whose advantages, it was estimated, would probably be nullified by improved Soviet defences from about 1965 onwards. Even an improved Blue Steel would not have been as advanced as the

American weapon. Originally designated GAM-87A, the new weapon was later given the name Skybolt.

After preliminary discussions with the Americans on the possibility of acquiring the weapon for Bomber Command, proposals for further development of Blue Steel were abandoned, although the Mk 1 version was pushed ahead as quickly as conditions permitted. The Skybolt saga, alas, was to become a classic example of political horse-trading and military ineptitude seldom experienced in British public life before or since, with deliberate misrepresentation by sections of the British Press for ulterior political motives.

The arrival of Thor in 1957 had introduced an era of rapid development in missile technology which was not confined to the scientific laboratories of the West. Russia was also active in this field and it had become evident that she was developing a ballistic missile force at top priority, which would have the ability to attack targets anywhere in Europe with medium-range missiles. This was to be followed by a programme for the development of intercontinental missiles, capable of attacks against the North American continent. America, more conscious of the potential of missiles than most countries, speeded up the development of a massive radar warning system, designed to detect and give warning of missile attack over the polar route to North America. Two enormous radar tracking stations were constructed at Thule in Greenland and Clear in Alaska. These were in addition to another radar chain stretching across Canada and America from coast to coast, which gave warning of attack from manned aircraft, the DEW (Distant Early Warning) line. The new organization, known as the Ballistic Missile Early Warning System (BMEWS), came into operational use in 1960. From its radars, at least 15 minutes warning could be obtained of the approach of intercontinental missiles fired from Russia against North America. Unfortunately, there was no comparable system in Europe, although the missile threat to Europe and Britain in particular was even greater. This deficiency was eventually corrected, but not until 1964, when the third station at Fylingdales in Yorkshire became operational.

It was vital that Bomber Command should have warning of missile attacks against America in order that suitable measures could be taken to protect, and subsequently launch, the V-bomber force and

111

Thor, since an attack on America would almost certainly have heralded an attack on the whole NATO Alliance. The V-bombers and Thor formed the only nuclear force permanently based the European side of the Atlantic capable of penetrating deep into Russia and striking important strategic targets. Moreover they would be the first to retaliate if a nuclear strike had been made on any member of the Alliance. SAC units were, of course, also based at certain stations in Britain, but on a rotational basis.

The control centre at Bomber Command Headquarters was eventually linked directly to NORAD at Colorado Springs — the control centre for the whole North American air defence organization. Bomber Command was thus able to share with Strategic Air Command all early warning information of attack, whether by manned aircraft or missiles, directed against America. Fylingdales was designed to give early warning of medium-range missiles directed at Europe, particularly the British Isles, and when completed it was planned to link Bomber Command, Fighter Command and NORAD with this new site, thereby providing radar cover over a vast area of the northern hemisphere. This plan eventually reached fruition in 1964, but from 1960 onwards, the warning obtainable from American sources was invaluable.

The years 1956 to 1959 were the formative years of Britain's independent nuclear deterrent. They were packed with activity, enthusiasm and hope, and there was uncompromising loyalty and devotion to the new force among all ranks serving in Bomber Command. During this period, the Commander-in-Chief, Air Marshal Sir Harry Broadhurst, provided the leadership needed and brought to many planning and policy conferences the benefit of his wide and varied experience. When his tour of duty ended in 1959 he handed over to Air Marshal Sir Kenneth Cross, who had for the previous three years been Air Officer Commanding No3 Group, operating Victors and Valiants. He came to the Command Headquarters with a detailed knowledge of aircraft, equipment and the operational capability of the bomber force but, even more important, he was acutely aware that ordinary standards of proficiency would not be good enough for Bomber Command in its nuclear deterrent role. His policy from the outset, therefore, was to create an organization second to none in efficiency and operational capability, as a demonstration to the world that Britain's independent nuclear deterrent was the equal in credibility, if not in numbers, of any other force.

The appointment of Sir Kenneth Cross took place at a time when a new era in the development of Bomber Command and its weapons was about to begin, and which held promise of stimulating and exacting tasks ahead. As it turned out, there were also to be frustrations and bitter disappointments for all those who had come to regard Bomber Command as Britain's greatest military achievement this century or, perhaps, of all time. It has certainly not been equalled since the Command was abolished in 1968. Nevertheless, during the years from 1960 to 1965, the Command reached the height of its power and influence and earned a reputation for efficiency, readiness and determination equal to any in the world.

The terms of the Commander-in-Chief's Directive in 1959 detailed four main roles for Bomber Command. The first and most important was its peace role, namely, to act as the principal British nuclear deterrent to global war; the second, to reinforce overseas commands as required; the third, to assist NATO or other allied forces; and the fourth, in the event of nuclear war, to destroy those targets allocated to it by the British Chiefs of Staff. At that time strategic nuclear targets were decided solely by the British Chiefs of Staff on the recommendation of a special committee in the Ministry of Defence, but the target plan was co-ordinated with Strategic Air Command for the very sensible reason that by so doing each made the maximum use of the other's knowledge and obtained the maximum coverage of, and concentration on, priority targets.

An important point to note in the directive is recognition of the flexibility of the bomber force by its assignment to secondary roles where conventional bombs were likely to be used. Throughout its existence Bomber Command retained this capacity, though it has not always been recognized or properly understood outside the Royal Air Force. Training for conventional warfare had figured prominently in the Command's activities since World War II, and on becoming Britain's nuclear deterrent it was able to undertake both roles without difficulty. Indeed, Valiants featured largely in the successful air attacks carried out during the Suez campaign, whatever the disasters and failures that characterized that unfortunate episode in British history. Even up to the middle of 1968, Bomber Command represented a most powerful conventional air striking force, capable of being deployed rapidly to any part of the world.

But it was in 1962, just when the Command was reaching the peak of its operational efficiency with a mixed force of missiles and manned bombers, that a unique opportunity occurred to assess its deterrent posture, alert and readiness state, and communications system in a truly realistic atmosphere which had not previously been experienced and has not recurred. The eventful week ending 28th October 1962, brought to a climax a drama that had been unfolding over a period of months. America, as the world now knows, watched events in Cuba very closely and with mounting apprehension from July onwards. The development of that unhappy island as a hostile base for the deployment of offensive nuclear missiles on America's doorstep was something no reasonable person could imagine the American Administration tolerating for very long. The Russian offensive missiles deployed, or destined to be deployed, in Cuba were short-range weapons which could be used only against targets on the North American continent, and it was equally clear that they were capable of carrying nuclear warheads. Russian defensive surface-to-air missiles (SAM) were also being deployed in Cuba. The incident in May 1960, when Gary Powers, flying an American U-2 reconnaissance aircraft was shot down by Soviet SAM missiles, was very much to the forefront in discussions on air strategy on both sides of the Atlantic from 1960 onwards.

The Defence Ministry in London and Bomber Command staff watched anxiously during this tense period and speculated on how America might react. By 20th October the situation had deteriorated so seriously and rapidly that the Commander-in-Chief kept in continuous communication with the Air Ministry in London and with Strategic Air Command Headquarters at Omaha, Nebraska. During the weekend of 25th October, as tension mounted, SAC informed Bomber Command that it had increased its readiness state from alert condition 3 to 2. Fortunately, Bomber Command stations were involved in one of their frequent alert and readiness exercises, so that they were able to take certain preliminary measures as a matter of

114

routine, in case the situation deteriorated. On the evening of 26th October, the Commander-in-Chief, Air Marshal Sir Kenneth Cross, called the duty operations officer on the telephone to say that he had decided to allow the exercise to proceed and to retain the existing readiness state for the time being. In Bomber Command, it was mandatory for operations rooms to be manned twenty-four hours a day, so that if it had been necessary to change the alert states of the force, quite apart from exercise requirements, this could have been done smoothly and efficiently.

In the early hours of Saturday morning, 27th October, the Commander-in-Chief went to the operations room to discuss the exercise with his senior staff members and to hear the latest news from America, in particular President Kennedy's statements on the gravity of the situation and Russian reaction to American warnings. The C-in-C decided to increase the readiness state of the force, purely as part of the training exercise. The necessary instructions were given over the broadcast telephone system; within seconds orders were being flashed simultaneously to all stations and were just as promptly obeyed.

In the War Room, the indicator board recording previous orders and changes in readiness states showed that the latest orders had been complied with and Groups and Stations had acknowledged their new instructions. The officer in charge of the operations centre reported all communications networks functioning correctly. There had not, so far, been any feature in the events of the precious twenty-four hours that had not been practised many times before, but on this occasion there was a slightly more realistic air about the proceedings. Both the Thor missile force and the V-bombers were at fifteen minutes readiness. The bombers were nearer to Russia by about five hours than aircraft of Strategic Air Command based in America and Thor's reaction time from the order to launch until impact on target in Russia was about twenty-five minutes. This represented a very impressive megatonnage (230 megatons on 230 targets to be precise), most of which would have reached their assigned targets if orders had been given to attack. What is more important, the Russians knew it too.

Time slipped slowly by and it was gratifying to all those present to watch the speed and precision with which Bomber Command reacted to changes in readiness states, and the skill with which full operational capability was maintained. Perhaps one of the most impressive features of the exercise was the achievement of the Thor crews in bringing all sixty missiles to operational standby; a feat which few would have thought possible only a year earlier.

The Command maintained a high state of readiness throughout Saturday and Sunday, listening to the "Voice of America" on radio sets in their homes, in offices, or on the dispersal platforms. A most interesting, comprehensive and up-to-date account of events in Washington was maintained continuously, including the dramatic and climactic contents of Khrushchev's letter of 38th October, in which he stated "In order to eliminate as rapidly as possible the conflict which endangers the cause of peace ... the Soviet Government has given a new order to dismantle the arms which have been described as offensive and to crate them and return them to the Soviet Union". It was all over. The crisis had passed. The exercise was finished and the Commander-in-Chief quietly ordered the force to be relaxed to a lower state of readiness. It is doubtful if more than a handful of people outside Bomber Command had any idea of what had happened.

It had been a tense, but stimulating experience and one which gave Bomber Command an unrivalled opportunity to study the whole system for controlling the V-bomber force in an emergency. Throughout it all, no one really felt that the deterrent would fail when put to the test; nor, apparently, did those who controlled the destinies of the free world in that anxious week. If there had been no deterrent, or if it had failed to sustain the philosophy of deterrence on which British and American defence policies were based, another world war might have started. The fact that the deterrent succeeded, surely justified the concept to the full. Moreover, the British contribution in terms of Thor and the V-bomber force, so close to the Russian home-land, was obviously not entirely ignored by Russia in reaching her decision to withdraw the missiles from Cuba. It will be remembered that the combined Allied Bomber Forces rained down more than two million tons of bombs on Germany in the six years of war 1939-45, devastating almost every major town or industrial complex from the Rhine to Berlin and from the Baltic to the Swiss border. In 1962, Bomber Command alone could have despatched the equivalent of 230 million tons in one raid, enough to destroy every major city or centre of population in the entire Soviet Union. A sobering thought.

Perhaps the outstanding lesson of the October crisis was the value of a mixed force of aircraft and missiles, assuming that a suitable warning system to track the approach of enemy missiles is also available. Such a force gives a commander freedom of choice once the political decision to launch a nuclear response had been taken. In the Cuban crisis, ample strategic warning in the form of a build-up in political tension was available in addition to tactical warning from the DEW line and BMEWS. Unfortunately, Britain no longer had plans for ground-based ballistic missiles, but was pinning her hopes for the future of the British independent nuclear deterrent on Skybolt, the American air-launched ballistic missile which promised to incorporate all the best features of manned aircraft and ballistic missiles. The nuclear warhead for the missile was to be designed and produced in Britain, so that there would be no question of restrictions on the handling or control of the warheads, such as had been imposed on Thor. The independence of Bomber Command as Britain's deterrent, it was hoped, would always be assured.

It had been suggested earlier in 1962, that Britain might consider acquiring Polaris submarines similar to those in operation in the United States Navy as an alternative to Skybolt, but the idea was dismissed on the grounds of cost. To produce a force of submarine-launched missiles with equivalent capability to that of Bomber Command (230 megatons), would have required at least twenty submarines at a cost considered beyond Britain's ability to pay in the economic climate then prevailing. The proposal, nevertheless, remained uppermost in the minds of Lord Mountbatten and Sir Solly Zuckerman, whose chief concern was with restoring the image of a rapidly declining Navy. There was no "doctrinal vacuum" as some amateur strategists have suggested in recent years, it was inter-Service rivalry and economic decline that were the main considerations which forced Britain to adopt the nuclear and defence policies that emerged from 1962 onwards.

The Royal Air Force – and Bomber Command in particular – had the unenviable task of maintaining a nuclear deterrent force, which presented unique problems of security, safety and technology, demanding the undivided attention of all those connected with it, and needed neither the attentions of snipers from the other Services nor the antics of the anti-nuclear lobby. Inter-Service rivalry was rife in the corridors of Whitehall, despite the efforts of a dedicated few who believed in joint co-operation. On his return to naval duty after an extended absence during which he had handed India back to the Indians, Admiral Earl Mountbatten of Burma advanced rapidly to absolute power and influence in Whitehall. In 1955 he became First Sea Lord and head of the Navy, a post he held for four years, during which he fought resolutely to restore the strength of the Navy at the expense of the other two Services. While the Army and Air Force suffered repeated cuts in successive defence budgets and the cancellation of new equipment, the Navy was able to maintain its share of the budgets — and even increase it. Mountbatten forced through the commando carrier and the idea of the carrier task force, guided missile ships and nuclear submarines. Such was his prestige, power and influence, that only token resistance was offered by the other two Chiefs of Staff.

Having completed four years as head of the Navy, Mountbatten moved on to become the first Chief of Defence Staff, a newly created post in the Ministry of Defence. Normally the tour for such duty is three years, but Mountbatten remained in Whitehall for a continuous tour of duty extending over ten years. On assuming his role, Admiral Mountbatten brought his friend Sir Solly Zuckerman to the Ministry with him as chief scientific adviser. It was hardly surprising that he supported his master on such topics as strategic nuclear forces, aircraft carriers and their strike aircraft which were calculated to further the aims of the Navy. The RAF had a difficult time in countering attacks from many quarters within Whitehall on a variety of issues, the outcome of which did little to further the interests of the defence and security of the country.

From 1962, in the run-up to the general election in 1964, antagonism towards the nuclear deterrent and Bomber Command increased in intensity and culminated in one of the most squalid political deceptions ever witnessed in the British political arena. Accusations and promises were made for the purposes of vote catching, which an indifferent electorate accepted as truthful. It was not until after the election that the truth about the campaign against the nuclear deterrent was revealed, and it became clear that Labour had little intention of honouring promises made to their voluble left wing.

9

Skybolt Saga

The cancellation of Blue Streak and Blue Steel Mk2 was occasioned mainly by the prospect of obtaining Skybolt from America. An air-launched ballistic missile which could be operated by the very efficient Vulcan and Victor V-bombers from existing bases in the United Kingdom and overseas, offered a most attractive and effective weapons system, and one that could prolong the life of the V-bomber force well into the 1970s and beyond, thus utilizing to the full the world network of bases on which much capital investment had been expended in the previous decade.

Technologically, an air-launched ballistic missile was entirely feasible and had been discussed as a future weapons system as early as 1954. American scientists were well ahead with design studies and an experimental missile was actually fired from a B-47 Stratojet bomber in 1957, to test compatibility between manned aircraft and ballistic missiles. By 1958, three American companies, under a project known as Bold Orion, began a detailed investigation into problems likely to be encountered in producing an operational weapons system using air-launched ballistic missiles. Further test launchings made from B-47s by the Martin Company confirmed theoretical calculations that launching ballistic missiles from an aircraft was not only possible, but offered the prospect of advantages over other forms of delivery systems, including greater mobility, flexibility, dispersal and security. If a missile, or missiles, could be carried on existing types of aircraft such as B-47 Stratojet, B-52 Stratofortress, Victor and Vulcan bombers, the United States Air Force and the Royal Air Force would have a new and revolutionary weapon system against which there was no known defence. Launched from heights of 40,000 feet, or above, the range and payload of an air-launched missile would be relatively greater than existing surface-launched missiles, since they would start their journey in the upper atmosphere outside enemy defences, with an initial high velocity. Less thrust would therefore be required for a given range and weight.

From preliminary tests it appeared that such a weapon could be made small enough for two and perhaps four to be carried by one aircraft. This represented an enormous saving in overheads in addition to other advantages. Operating from a ground or airborne alert posture, missiles could be directed against pre-planned targets or on an opportunity basis. The weapons could be mounted on pylons under the wings, thereby freeing bomb-bays for other weapons, nuclear or conventional, or for additional fuel. A whole permutation of systems was possible and the vulnerability of the weapons, or aircraft, was no greater — and probably less — than ground-launched ballistic missiles from silos, or Polaris missiles from submarines. Neither of the latter systems, of course, had any flexibility whatever, for they cannot be used for any purpose other than to pose a nuclear deterrent. Both land and sea environments have limitations that are well known, but the air is free and limitless; it knows no barriers and aircraft patrolling in the vast uncharted areas of space outside enemy radar surveillance, armed with nuclear ballistic missiles, would be less vulnerable, less expensive and more effective than any other offensive nuclear weapons systems that Britain could acquire and afford.

In short, the air-launched ballistic missiles offered a combination of reliability, flexibility and precision which are the main requisites of manned bombers, with the superlative performance and rapid retaliatory capabilities of ballistic missiles. The Americans were far advanced in developing both ground-based missiles, and Polaris missiles for firing from submarines, in addition to their large bomber force, and justification for another weapons system, whatever its advantages, was obviously going to be hard to establish, especially if it appeared to supersede or clash with the US Navy's requirements for the Polaris missile. The Navy lobby in America was even more powerful than in Britain. The "mixed force" combination of ground-launched missiles and manned bombers was operated by Britain until Thor reached the end of its programmed operational life in 1963.

There was no planned replacement for Thor, and Blue Streak had already been cancelled. So Britain's requirement for Skybolt was, therefore, even more urgent and necessary than that of the United States Air Force. Those who were concerned lest Britain should lose her ability to mount strategic bombing operations, were delighted when it was announced on 26th May 1959, that the Douglas Aircraft Corporation, the firm that produced the successful Thor in record time, had been awarded a contract to produce an air-launched ballistic missile for the US Air Force.

Bomber Command had become interested in a weapons system of this kind in 1957, but the first real step forward came in 1958 when a study group concluded "The hypersonic strategic air-to-surface missile under study in America and planned for introduction into Strategic Air Command about 1963, is superior to anything we could produce in a similar period in the United Kingdom". The group recommended an immediate assessment of the weapons system for compatibility with the V-bombers and, in 1959, the Ministry of Defence accepted the implications of their recommendations and made proposals for formal acquisition by Bomber Command. Representatives from the Ministry of Supply, Handley Page and Avro visited the United States in June 1959 to study design proposals for the installation of Skybolt on Mk 2 Vulcans and Victors.

There were no insuperable difficulties, though certain modifications to the aircraft were considered essential. As a result of the team's report in December 1959, the Minister of Defence asked America formally for a joint USAF/RAF project. On 13th April 1960, the Minister of Defence announced in the Commons that there was much merit to be said for buying Skybolt, which, to those familiar with its potential, seemed to be a gross understatement. To air strategists it was something long dreamed of and to economists it was the cheapest and most logical course for Britain to adopt. The country could not afford ground-based missiles in hardened silos, or a large enough force of expensive and inflexible Polaris submarines with their costly bases and support facilities, which from a cost effectiveness point of view was the least desirable system. So Skybolt emerged as probably the best solution for maintaining an efficient deterrent at a cost within Britain's capacity to meet.

On 6th June 1960, a memorandum of understanding was signed in Washington between the Minister of Defence and the US Secretary of Defense, for the supply of Skybolt for Bomber Command. Earlier in 1960, the first information publicly released on the new system described it as a "two-stage, solid propellent, hypersonic ballistic missile with a range of about 1,000 miles, equipped with astro-inertial guidance and capable of carrying a large yield nuclear payload in a re-entry vehicle". It was acknowledged by most scientific and engineering experts in Britain and the United States that the technological know-how required to produce such a weapon was well within the capabilities of American companies engaged in missile research and development. Solid propellents made it possible for the missile to be made much smaller than anything of comparable performance so far produced and, although the guidance system was complicated and presented problems, many similar problems had been overcome in other projects. The star tracker system proposed for the astro-inertial guidance unit had already been tried in an air-breathing missile and many other proven components and techniques could also be used.

But, even at this early stage of development, voices were being raised in the United States Congress in support of a reduction in the number and variety of missiles, in being or under development. While it was agreed that a balanced nuclear deterrent force consisting of manned aircraft and ballistic missiles was highly desirable, another system appeared to be duplicating what was already available. Strategic Air Command had over 900 long-range aircraft in addition to Atlas, Titan and Minuteman missiles, but no one raised any strong objection, apparently, when the United States Navy added Polaris to the already gross over-kill potential of SAC. Curiously enough, proposals for further development of Skybolt and its application to nuclear-powered aircraft, or the B-70 Mach 3 bomber, which would have been a logical advance towards putting the American nuclear deterrent into space, received a cool reception. Many senior officers in Strategic Air Command openly confessed that decisions taken by the Congress, or sometimes in the Pentagon, were not always based on sound military appreciations; a state of affairs not uncommon in Britain.

On 20th June 1960, the Cabinet approved a Ministry of Defence Paper on the whole concept of Skybolt for Bomber Command and authorized the Minister to sign financial and technical agreements with the United States. In August, the first meeting of Britain's Skybolt Board in London was followed by a meeting of Anglo-American planners which cleared the way for the establishment of a British Project Office at Wright-Patterson Air Force Base, to work alongside their USAF colleagues, thus completing a basic organization for advancing British interests in Skybolt. This was a similar procedure to that used so successfully in the Thor programme. By this time it had been decided to confine Skybolt to the Vulcan Mk 2, because mounting the weapons on Victors would have required large and expensive modifications.

By March 1961, doubts were being expressed, by certain elements in this country, about the reliability and good faith of the United States to supply the weapon at all, despite the solemn agreements entered into less than a year previously. During a debate in the House of Commons on the 1960 Defence White Paper, the Minister of Defence felt obliged to give the House assurances that he had signed a memorandum with the United States which had no strings attached; Skybolt, he said, would be delivered in the promised time scale and would be cheaper than any comparable weapon which Britain could produce or acquire. But a minority was already marshalling its forces and accusing America of bad faith, almost before the ink was dry on the signed agreement. They used the occasion to revive old arguments, based on ignorance and emotion, that we should opt out of the nuclear business altogether and leave all bombing to the Americans; which would, of course, have relegated Britain to the status of a third class power even more quickly than successive Labour Governments achieved in their terms of office between 1964 and 1978.

Early in April 1961, by way of confirmation of America's determination to go ahead with the Skybolt project, President Kennedy called for an additional fifty million dollars in his defence budget, to speed the Skybolt development programme, a proposal generally welcomed by most well-informed people, both in America and in this country.

By February 1962, British plans had advanced to a stage where

Bomber Command was able to attach a trials team to Avro at Woodford, where Vulcan Mk 2 aircraft were being built to carry Skybolt. In May, a trials team was also established at Eglin Air Force Base in Florida, where trial launchings from B-52 Stratofortress and Vulcan aircraft were planned to take place. In fact, only a week before the team arrived, the first launch had been carried out from a B-52 over Cape Canaveral. This test had limited objectives, confined mainly to launch and motor functioning. The weapon released successfully from the parent aircraft, first stage light-up occurred and pitch-up was successful; but the second stage failed owing to ignition trouble. For a maiden flight of a completely new weapon the results were encouraging, fully justifying the confidence shown in the system by all concerned. The US Secretary of Defense described the missile as a highly complex weapon operating in a new environment with many development problems to be overcome. He said he was less optimistic than either the USAF or the manufacturers, but if development problems could be solved he felt that promised delivery dates could be met.

The second test took place on 29th June and again release was satisfactory, but this time the first stage failed; once again ignition trouble was the cause. The whole ignition system was redesigned in a matter of two months, ready for the next test on 13th September. This time, the signal for light-up was not transmitted at all and first stage failure resulted. Round four was released on 25th September; both motors ignited satisfactorily, but thrust reversal occurred prematurely after ignition causing loss of range. Nevertheless, this was the most successful test so far in the series, and there was indication that problems were being overcome. The fifth weapon, released on 28th November, was intended to be a fully guided test using design guidance and control systems. Unfortunately this test also was only partially successful, despite the fact that pre-launch indications were good; the star tracker astro-inertial system functioned correctly, initial release was perfect, first stage light-up occurred as programmed and pitch-up was satisfactory. But instability was observed on the subsequent climb and, although first stage separation, second stage ignition and firing were all successful, the missile became erratic and failed to continue on a programmed flight trajectory, owing to malfunctioning of the flight control system.

There was, of course, adverse comment from those who had questioned the wisdom of the project in the first place, and positive delight, especially in this country, from those who fervently hoped the system would not work. It was reported in some American newspapers that President Kennedy had already decided that the USAF did not need Skybolt anyway and that its cancellation would help his plans to reduce defence expenditure. The extraordinary thing was that no mention appears to have been made in official circles of the fact that at least three failures had occurred from six firings of the first Mark of Polaris missile — there might well have been others. Polaris A2 had four failures out of six, and the A3 six failures out of six. When one considers the numerous failures that occurred at Cape Canaveral in the early days of the missile and space programme, including failures of the most successful of all missiles, Thor, it seems strange that there should have been so much enthusiasm for scrapping Skybolt, when it gave promise of being a highly successful weapon despite initial setbacks. It became abundantly clear later that technological difficulties were not the primary cause of Skybolt's demise. Other influences were at work on both sides of the Atlantic.

On 10th December 1962, while a reappraisal of Skybolt was being made in America, Secretary of Defense McNamara left Washington for talks with the British Minister of Defence in London. The British Government had, at that time, made it plain that Britain wanted Skybolt, and substitutes would be unacceptable. One Washington newspaper may have opened the curtain a chink on American defence policy when it reported McNamara as saying that Skybolt would be nice to have, but was not essential. This attitude, the paper concluded, completely ignored solemn agreements entered into with Britain, and the fact that she had staked her nuclear future on Skybolt. An agonizing reappraisal of Anglo-American relations was forecast if the Administration decided to cancel the project, so attention focused on the forthcoming meeting between President Kennedy and Prime Minister Macmillan in the Bahamas on 19th December 1962.

During this dramatic period, from March until December, considerable progress had been made in trials in Bomber Command with dummy Skybolt missiles on Vulcans. Releases had been carried out successfully, full compatibility tests had been completed and a trials team – now firmly established at Eglin Air Force Base – had assured Bomber Command officers on numerous occasions during Staff visits that the programme was going well and on time. The Commander-in-Chief, Air Marshal Sir Kenneth Cross, with a team from Headquarters Bomber Command, visited Eglin and the Douglas Company in October, and were impressed with progress at all stages of development in the Skybolt programme. It was stated that no technical difficulties that could not be overcome had been encountered and the date for introduction of the missile into service would be met. Bomber Command had no reason whatever to suspect that there were defects which might cause the project to be reviewed. On the contrary, they were busily engaged in working out operating procedures for the new weapon and introducing training schemes for air and ground crews. But they were not fully aware of the political intrigue taking place on the other side of the Atlantic, and were taken by surprise by what happened in those fateful days before Christmas 1962.

Secretary of Defense McNamara's visit to London in December, it was thought, might indicate a cut-back in American orders for Skybolt, but no one suspected that Britain's interests would be affected, and there was certainly no hint that the project would be cancelled. Only two days previously the trials team at Eglin had been given authority to purchase caravans as living accommodation for families on their way out from Britain to join their husbands, and approval had also been given for the construction of a school for the children. But three or four days prior to the Nassau meeting, it became clear that something sensational was about to break. The *Manchester Guardian* of 13th December reported that the Minister of Defence had made it plain to Mr McNamara in the strongest terms that Skybolt was of the greatest importance to Britain, and went on to comment on the Secretary of Defense's statement that "all five tests had been failures". The *Guardian* wryly observed that this was perhaps a slight exaggeration.

Up to this time there had never been any suggestion that Britain was again considering Polaris as an alternative, although there had been signs of lobbying, and it was known that Zuckerman favoured Polaris and he was in Nassau. It had been seriously contended in one

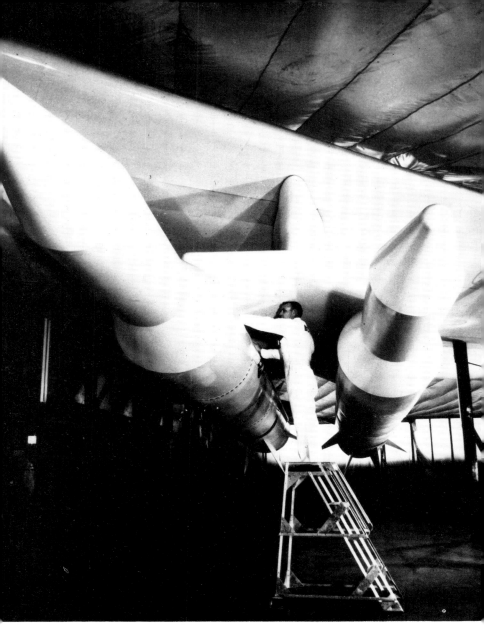

Skybolt, the American air-launched ballistic missile.

A Boeing B-52 Stratofortress could carry four Skybolts.
A Vulcan with a mock-up of the Skybolt missiles.

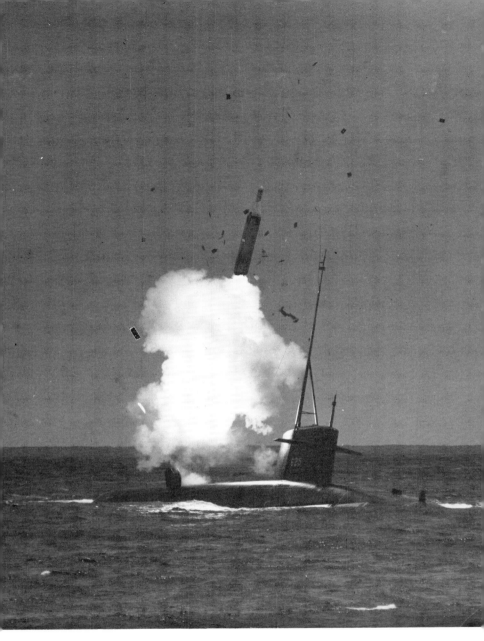

The trial launch of a Polaris A2 missile from the nuclear-powered USS
Henry Clay off Cape Kennedy, 20th April 1964.

Firing of the first Polaris missile from HMS *Resolution* off the Florida coast in February, 1968.

Tomahawk cruise missile in a trial sub-surface launch from a submarine off California.

HMS *Resolution*, one of four submarines of her class.

HMS *Revenge*, Britain's fourth nuclear submarine, at Port Canaveral, Cape Kennedy, during a month's visit to the USA in 1970 for test Polaris firings.

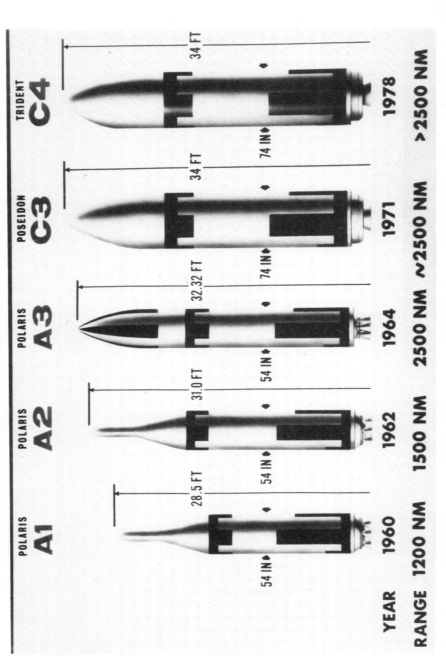

Fleet Ballistic Missiles.

academic institution's magazine that Polaris submarines would be more acceptable to the British people than missiles to be dropped from bomber aircraft! The prejudiced thinking that surrounds almost every topic connected with air power, and particularly offensive air power, in this country is unbelievable, and is rivalled only by the subterfuges of military opportunists who believe that tradition has something to do with military requirements. The cries that went up from moralists at the end of World War II were heard again, and were repeated with almost monotonous regularity on radio, television and in a small section of the Press. It was, apparently, acceptable to starve civil populations to death by naval blockade, or incinerate them with naval nuclear missiles, but immoral to bomb munitions factories, aircraft factories, tank factories or, most important of all, submarine yards, most of which happen to be located in large cities or ports, where civilian populations inevitably were at risk.

Many people in this country also failed to appreciate the totally different concept of operations with Skybolt from bases in this country, where aircraft were in launch position minutes after take-off, whereas, operating from bases in the United States, SAC had to fly for about five or six hours to reach launch areas. It was a similar situation to Thor. Bomber Command was in an ideal position to operate the weapon, SAC was not, and first strike in any nuclear conflict would have to come from Bomber Command. We would, in effect, have had the primary deterrent weapons system in the West. This may have had some bearing on the decision taken later, but it was not the paramount reason for the cancellation of Skybolt.

On 13th December, President Kennedy, commenting on the Skybolt controversy which was by now widespread, said that the weapon was "the most sophisticated imaginable; to fire a missile from a plane at high speed to hit a target 1,000 miles away required the most advanced technology". He thought it was "the kind of engineering that was beyond the United States technological capability". This sort of assessment might have been expected from a simple ex-sailor, but from a President of the United States it was an insult to the men who had demonstrated such skill in scientific and technological developments in aeronautics, electronics, space, and atomic physics.

On 17th December, in a broadcast and television interview just before he left for the Bahamas and his crucial meeting with Mr Macmillan, Kennedy gave an unmistakable hint that Skybolt was doomed. By 20th December it was dead. In its place, as a sort of consolation prize, Britain was to get Polaris missiles, which even the Navy did not want, because they thought it might jeopardize the carrier programme. It did. The Polaris programme later escaped cancellation in the 1965 Defence Review on the grounds that it was too far advanced in production to be abolished. Britain was, therefore, saddled with a very expensive and not wholly effective weapons system; one which, by itself, did not constitute a deterrent — independent or otherwise. Today it is a pitiful contribution to a kind of collective deterrent operated by NATO, and the least credible or effective of all the nuclear deterrents in the armouries of the United States, Soviet Union or France.

The *Washington Post* came nearest to the truth when it stated on 21st December that the five "so-called" failures cited by the Kennedy Administration as the main cause of Skybolt's cancellation had nothing to do with the final decision to abandon it. Economic and political reasons were suggested as the principal factors and a desire by the Kennedy Government to level off defence expenditure. But, if this was so, why not scrap, or cut back on Polaris, or Minuteman, or some of the other missile programmes, for there were no solemn agreements for the supply of these systems to Britain? The unanimous and expert advice of the United States Chiefs of Staff, Strategic Air Command and the best scientists and engineers engaged on the project was that Skybolt should be continued; but their advice was rejected and the project was cancelled on the grounds, the President said, that America did not have the technological knowledge to make the weapon work. But the last word was to come from those engaged on developing the project, and they gave their answer in unequivocal terms less than a week later.

On 22nd December the sixth and last round was fired, despite the announcement that the project had been cancelled. It was an out-standing success, within the parameters set, by travelling a distance of 900 miles down the range with all systems working satisfactorily. With a development programme similar to that allowed for other systems, Skybolt would have been a success. No one seriously believes now that either the Douglas Company or the United States Air Force would have risked the ultimate humiliation that another failure would have brought, if they had not had complete confidence in the weapon and the ability of their engineers and scientists to produce it to the required specifications. Many of those who attended the Nassau meeting from both countries must have wished that test number six had never taken place. Even after it was all over, there were some who tried desperately to discredit the results of the test and even accused the United States Air Force of issuing false information. Most people just shook their heads and pondered on a remarkable train of events. They had heard many reasons advanced for cancelling Skybolt, and they were to hear others from sections of the Press that were even more bizarre and inaccurate, but it was already plain that technical difficulties were not the primary cause of Skybolt's cancellation.

Militarily the loss of Skybolt was a severe blow to Britain and to the Royal Air Force. It is now generally agreed that the main reasons for not continuing with this weapon were political and economic, with the assistance of some high-powered lobbying by individuals and groups in this country who wished to see an end to Skybolt or any other weapon if it was to be operated by the Royal Air Force. Many senior officers in the United States and in this country, together with distinguished scientists and engineers with no axe to grind, agreed that Skybolt was an imaginative and entirely feasible project, which would have conferred enormous advantages on Britain's nuclear deterrent for probably two decades. Its urgency in the United States was not as pressing as in Britain, but its strategic application and further development potential were crystal clear to those who had studied strategic bombardment seriously and understood the implications for the future. Bomber Command had even gone so far as to examine Skybolt in operational concepts ten or twenty years ahead, when the Vulcans might be reaching the end of their design life. Vulcans and United States B-52s are still in service today, and if Skybolt had been produced it would have been the least vulnerable and most effective missile system in the world.

If, as has been suggested, one of the reasons for cancelling Skybolt was political, then the most likely explanation was the Kennedy Administration's opposition to the development or continuation of nuclear deterrents by other countries. This even though Britain had operated her own independent deterrent for more than six years and had contributed as much, if not more, to the discovery and development of atomic power for military purposes as any other nation. It was well known that a faction in this country, including Zuckerman and Labour politicians, agreed with the Kennedy decision to cancel Skybolt, and Britain's acceptance of four Polaris submarines was seen as the lesser of a number of possible evils. It ensured that Britain's days as an independent nuclear power were over, since by no stretch of the imagination could a force of four or five submarines be considered an independent nuclear deterrent to aggression by the Soviet Union. McNamara is on record as saying "independent nuclear deterrents are dangerous and unnecessary", referring, of course, to those of Britain and France.

If cost was a deciding factor in cancelling Skybolt, it is pertinent to examine some figures. It is well-nigh impossible, so long after the event and with so little development completed on the missile, to arrive at a precise assessment of what the ultimate cost would have been. Bearing in mind the large number of weapons originally intended for Strategic Air Command and Bomber Command, running into many hundreds, the long term cost per missile could have been less than for any other system so far produced. It is well known that projects such as these tend to become more costly, owing to price rises, as development and production programmes progress, but this principle applies to nearly all systems in most countries. Few systems have fallen in price over original estimates, and Skybolt would have been no exception. It would almost certainly have followed the pattern of previous and contemporary systems, including Britain's Polaris submarines, which escalated well above the original estimated costs.

It must be stated in all fairness that the American Government did offer to hand over the Skybolt project to Britain if she were prepared to continue development and pay for it. Britain rejected the offer on the grounds of cost, an argument used against it by American politicians. Moreover, further development would have had to be carried out in America; it would have been unrealistic to move the project to Britain. This offer was therefore modified and America agreed to share with Britain any further costs of development, which were estimated at that time to be about $200 million (£70 million). The United States defence department had already spent $350 million on initial development, and this meant that Britain could have had a force of 100 Skybolt missiles for about £150 million, including her share of the remaining development costs. Compare this with £350 million spent on four Polaris submarines, representing a total strike capability of only sixty-four missiles, with never more than sixteen likely to be at sea ready for firing at any given time. To keep one submarine permanently on patrol, four are needed. There will always be one in dock for overhaul at periodic intervals, one on the way out to, and one on the way back, from the patrol area, and one unserviceable for modification, repair or routine inspection. It is possible that at certain times two submarines might be on patrol, but this could not be guaranteed.

It was estimated that the cost of the four submarines would probably rise to between £450 and £500 million by 1970, a staggering sum to pay for such a small nuclear capability, which did not pose a credible deterrent. Even when deployed operationally, Polaris submarines spend most of their lives in dock or in transit to and from patrol areas; only a small proportion is spent on active duty, and this represents one of the most uneconomical, inflexible and costly systems of all. Nor are these disadvantages entirely offset by claims that when at sea, Polaris is the least vulnerable system. This may be true today, but is unlikely to apply later in the 'eighties. The loss of one submarine means the irreparable loss of sixteen missiles, and nothing could be more vulnerable than a nuclear submarine in dock. One need only take a look at Faslane and remember Scapa Flow!

What of the other weapons systems available in America in 1962, when Britain was offered Polaris, bearing in mind her special geographical position, the basis of her defence policy and the fact that she had made no arrangements whatever to provide an alternative weapon from British designs? Indeed, because of the Government's confidence in Skybolt and the enormously increased power it would confer on the deterrent from the mid-'sixties for at least two decades, Britain had cancelled all other projects that might have been developed. Bomber Command had only Blue Steel, a short-range, stand-off missile, quite unsuitable for development as an air-launched ballistic missile in the same category as Skybolt.

There were several other American weapon systems available from which a choice might have been made. Of the ground-launched missiles, Atlas and Titan were the most advanced. Atlas was an intercontinental ballistic missile designed in the late 'forties, and modified many times before emerging in 1957 as a single stage rocket with two boosters, capable of carrying a large yield warhead. It became operational in 1959, but by then it was partly outmoded by the more efficient Titan, and both were inferior to the new solid-fuelled Minuteman missile just coming into service.

Minuteman, smaller, lighter and more efficient than either of the other two, was designed for installation in deep concrete silos, capable of withstanding all but a direct hit from powerful nuclear weapons. It could be launched within seconds from silos and had a higher reliability factor than any other missile, and was more accurate. It could be fired by remote control, singly or in salvo, needed less maintenance and was cheaper than Atlas or Titan.

Polaris was also a solid-fuelled missile with a range of 1,200 miles in earlier versions, extending to 2,800 miles in later models. The submarines from which they were designed to be launched were nuclear powered and represented an enormous capital outlay, accounting for the high cost of the weapons system as a whole. Nevertheless, only Polaris and Minuteman were really suitable for British purposes. It was estimated at the time that Minuteman would have cost just over £1 million per missile installed in concrete silos, but this figure would almost certainly have been less, eventually, following America's decision to order more than 1,000 of them for her own use. The cost of one Polaris submarine fully equipped with sixteen missiles was stated to be about £90 million, representing £5½ million per missile installed in launch tubes in a submarine.

Thus, in 1962, the running costs per missile, including capital costs and five years operation, would have worked out at about £1¼ million for Minuteman (reducing to just under a million), £2 million for Skybolt and at least £5½ million for Polaris. Minuteman static in its concrete silo, can be maintained at a high state of readiness and has rapid reaction time, but cannot be used for any purpose other than as a nuclear deterrent or nuclear strike force. Polaris, in its nuclear submarine, is mobile when out of harbour and enjoys a high degree of invulnerability when in the depths of the ocean. But it is a sitting duck in dock and since it spends much of its time there, its overall invulnerability is in fact relatively low. Polaris also has no function other than nuclear deterrence or nuclear retaliatory strike in the event of war.

On all counts, and especially from a cost-effective point of view, a small force of four Polaris submarines to replace the V-bombers was the wrong choice for Britain. A better solution as a substitute for Skybolt would have been a force of at least seven Polaris submarines in addition to the V-bomber force, or a Hundred Minuteman missiles in hardened silos, retaining the V-bomber force and improving its capability in both the nuclear and conventional roles for as long as possible – it could have been into the 'eighties. The "mixed force" is a sound and credible strategic concept which, with the V-force and Minuteman, or Polaris, would have suited British defence strategy admirably.

It thus appears that cost-effectiveness could not have been a governing factor in determining Britain's future nuclear strike capability. One senior officer in Strategic Air Command probably summed up the whole sorry business when he said, "We would have liked Skybolt, but our Administration decided we did not need it. Kennedy was determined that you should not have it." Polaris was obtained as a consolation prize after extreme lobbying by Navy supporters on grounds which could only be described as traditional and sentimental. Following the Skybolt saga, Britain lost her nuclear leadership in Europe. France embarked on a six-year military programme to provide ground-based missiles, manned aircraft and Polaris-type submarines, for delivering nuclear weapons against strategic targets.

If Britain were to opt out of the nuclear business by the end of the 1980s, it would leave France free to assume the mantle Britain once wore. The RAF had been reduced almost to impotence by the cancellation of every long-range weapon system that came along after the V-bombers – Blue Streak, Blue Steel Mk 2, Skybolt and TSR-2.

135

It may yet be possible in the not too distant future for Britain and France to join forces and thereby save something of Britain's nuclear prestige. Both public and private industry in France have produced some of the finest aeronautical designs in the world, at less cost and in shorter time than comparable items could be produced in this country, but it would be naive to imagine that Britain could go in with France on any project on terms less than full economic and technological participation.

December 1962 marked a turning point in Britain's determination to maintain her own independent nuclear deterrent. Bomber Command was slowly eroded and eventually abolished, which was what the majority of the Labour Government and the Navy lobby wanted. Britain's military friends across the Atlantic and in Europe noted the change with regret, but not surprise.

10

The Anti-Nuclear Campaign

January 1963 was a bitterly cold month; one of the coldest in living memory. There was a special chill in that part of the Chilterns which, for more than thirty years, had been the Headquarters of Bomber Command. From its operations room in the last war Air Marshal Sir Arthur Harris, as he then was, directed the highly successful bomber offensive against Germany, and within its walls many historic decisions have been made; on 4th January 1963 another was added to the list.

The Commander-in-Chief, Air Marshal Sir Kenneth Cross, arrived at his office as usual on that bleak morning. His staff had been discussing the recent extraordinary events which had taken place during those critical days before Christmas and the likely effects of the Nassau decisions on the future of the Command. The weapon system they had planned so carefully, from which so much was expected, was no longer available. The only alternative was to examine, as a matter of great urgency, the possibility of operating the entire force at low-level as a means of penetrating enemy defences. It would be necessary to decide what modifications would be required to aircraft and equipment to enable the V-bombers to operate in the new role; what training should be introduced for the crews and what facilities were likely to be available at home or abroad for low-level flying training. It was estimated that it would be at least five years before the Polaris submarines would become available, and in the meantime Bomber Command would have to maintain Britain's nuclear deterrent.

It was extremely fortunate that only a year earlier the Staff had carried out a thorough reappraisal of the Valiant's chances of survival in penetrating vastly improved defences which, it had been estimated, would be available between 1963 and 1965. The Valiant, it will be remembered, was inferior to the other two types in some aspects of performance and did not have such effective electronic counter-measures equipment. Studies had confirmed the view that the Valiant could not long continue to survive at high altitude against the growing Russian air and ground defence systems, so it was decided to carry out extensive trials to assess its performance at low-level. Tests in Canada over terrain similar to that in Eastern Europe and the Soviet Union, in winter and summer, showed that the aircraft had an excellent performance in that role, and that existing navigation and bombing radars could be modified to meet requirements. The decision was taken to adopt the new tactics and the Valiant force was operational at low-level by the end of 1962.

This exercise proved invaluable in assessing the possibilities of switching the Vulcans and Victors to a similar role. Additional tests were completed without difficulty and showed that, with modifications to aircraft and equipment similar to those incorporated in the Valiants, low-level operations would be extremely effective for many years ahead. This technique is today used extensively by most strategic and tactical bomber forces, and new generation, high-performance aircraft, like the American F-111 and the French Mirage IV, were designed specifically to operate in this mode. Apart from its obvious advantages from the attacker's point of view, it put the defences completely on the wrong foot, since the sophisticated defence systems operational or projected, in the Soviet Union were designed for defence against high-level attack, and their whole organization would need to be re-orientated and largely redesigned to meet the new threat.

The necessary modifications to equipment, although complicated and lengthy, were duly completed, and a comprehensive low-level training programme devised for the crews. The Canadian Government made a handsome contribution by offering low-flying facilities over sparsely populated country which proved to be ideal. Facilities were also obtained in the Near East. No insuperable problems arose during the conversion training and it was possible to maintain the quick reaction alert (QRA) capability in an emergency. Blue Steel, the stand-off missile, was modified to enable it to be launched from high or low level and it is greatly to the credit of British scientific staffs and the

138

manufacturers that this feat was achieved by the time the squadron conversions had been completed.

One of the most important decisions of the Nassau Agreement which had far-reaching repercussions, was the assignment of the whole of Bomber Command to NATO. Written into the Agreement were certain safeguards which ensured that Bomber Command retained a measure of freedom to meet purely national requirements. It will be recalled that the Valiants were already assigned to the Supreme Allied Commander Europe (SACEUR) on terms similar to other air forces based on the Continent. This was Britain's contribution to SACEUR's nuclear strike force and as such it was entirely under his control. The V-bomber force, which formed by far the largest element of Bomber Command, had always been under national control, but the new terms of assignment placed it at SACEUR's disposal on the outbreak of war. In peace, Bomber Command was to work closely with Supreme Headquarters Allied Powers in Europe (SHAPE) for targeting, war planning, co-ordination of strikes and periodic exercises. Other organizational and operational functions, such as readiness states, deployment, dispersal and logistic support, including such things as aircraft, weapons and the bases from which the aircraft operated, both at home and abroad, remained under national control. This gave the United Kingdom Government the right to withdraw the whole or any part of the force to meet purely national commitments. It was recognized, of course, that such withdrawals would almost certainly be for operations in a conventional, rather than a nuclear, role.

The terms of assignment were duly ratified on 23rd May 1963, and from that date direct target co-ordination with SAC was discontinued. Instead, all targeting was planned with SHAPE, but Bomber Command still maintained its close ties with SAC and continued the practice of frequent exchange visits to discuss ideas on doctrine and tactics. SAC had no intention of giving up its bomber force, which formed an essential part of the United States mixed force of ground-launched missiles and manned aircraft operated by SAC while Polaris missiles were operated by the US Navy.

The autumn of 1963 saw the end of Air Marshal Sir Kenneth Cross's tour of duty as Commander-in-Chief, Bomber Command. He had been at the Headquarters for over four years, and before that had been a Group Commander for three years – a very long spell of duty in most exacting appointments, especially for one so dedicated to the task of providing the country's nuclear deterrent. To him must go most of the credit for the high regard in which the force was held by the majority of the people of Britain. He had seen it rise to the peak of its efficiency, influence and power, and under his dynamic leadership it had earned the admiration and respect of Air Forces all over the world. It never lacked invitations to send aircraft on visits to foreign countries, where its equipment and efficiency were the envy and admiration of all who saw them.

With Sir Kenneth's departure on 6th September 1963, went some indefinable and intangible asset which the Command was not to experience again. Bomber Command and the British independent nuclear deterrent had seen their finest hours. There were dark days ahead. The year 1964 was election year and, as it turned out, it was neither a happy nor a prosperous one for Bomber Command or the Royal Air Force.

No one looking back now could fail to recognize a distinct pattern in the propaganda directed against the nuclear deterrent and Bomber Command by people whose knowledge of nuclear weapons and the application of air power was, to say the least, suspect. But few then knew the real source of, or reason for, the carefully planned and timed assault. As the date of the election drew near, tirades against the nuclear deterrent were conducted on radio and television with monotonous regularity, using the grossest forms of misrepresentation imaginable. To those old enough to remember the war years and German propaganda, the technique must have appeared familiar. There was, apparently, no room for informed discussion with experts in military affairs and especially air matters. Fair play was abandoned and although some discerning members of the public had already recognized the true object of a thoroughly disreputable campaign, they had to wait until after the election for the truth to be revealed.

The recently appointed defence correspondent of *The Times* began to vent his wrath on Bomber Command and the nuclear deterrent in 1962. Commenting on a speech on nuclear strategy by Mr McNamara, 19 July 1962, he said that the British Government claimed there was no divergence of view between the British and American Governments, adding, "The RAF Bomber Command is so closely integrated with the American Strategic Air Command in its target planning that it hardly comes into the category of an independent deterrent". The use of the word "integrated" and the implied dependence on America injected into the sentence gave a totally erroneous impression. In fact, Bomber Command had never been integrated with Strategic Air Command for any purpose whatsoever. It had always enjoyed the closest co-operation with SAC in every field and exchanges on tactical doctrine, equipment and strategic planning were notable features of a very harmonious relationship, which the defence correspondent of *The Times* either ignored or did not understand, though he had been given the information during a visit to Headquarters Bomber Command for a briefing soon after he took up his new post.

Of course Bomber Command discussed strategic targets with SAC and worked out a co-ordinated attack plan for the obvious purpose of ensuring that the best possible advantage was obtained from the respective striking forces; but in no sense were they ever dependent on SAC or America for the operation of the British independent nuclear deterrent as posed by the V-bomber force of Bomber Command.

Soon after the formal announcement of the cancellation of Skybolt was made, the defence correspondent of *The Times* leapt on to the rostrum of the paper's centre pages with a feature article on "Britain without Skybolt". The following extract is an example of misrepresentation: "To anyone familiar with the evolution of American strategy in the past two years there is nothing surprising about the decision to abandon the Skybolt missile. Skybolt's programme of sixty-five airborne tests started with a depressing run of failures." It was of course, well known and confirmed by Mr McNamara himself that there had been five tests, some of which were partially successful. The sixth test was a complete success within the parameters set for it, and it is difficult to understand how anyone could possibly write that there had been sixty-five tests, unless it was done deliberately to strengthen a weak case in the hope that the statement would not be publicly refuted. Unfortunately it was not.

In the same article, the writer says of Bomber Command, "It could in theory be used independently, but it is probably even now incapable of penetrating Soviet anti-aircraft defences and it is certainly not a second strike weapon". What ignorance. At that time, Bomber Command had both Thor missiles and the V-bomber force, and there was no way that an inexperienced journalist could possibly calculate the ability of Bomber Command to penetrate Soviet defences without detailed knowledge of the capabilities and deployment of Soviet air and ground defence systems and the V-bombers' capabilities to penetrate them, unless he had access to Top Secret information, which he certainly did not have.

During his visit to Bomber Command in 1961, the problems of penetrating a modern defence system and how they might be overcome were explained to this correspondent. The presentation was, of course, governed by strict security regulations which prevented disclosure of either the Soviet defence system in detail or the V-bomber's countermeasures equipment. He left an indelible impression on those who met him, of a man obsessed with the theory that the best contribution Britain could make to the defence of this country and of Europe was to have more troops on the Rhine, armed with conventional weapons, and to abolish the Royal Air Force. In a second article on 9th January 1963, he reinforced his opinions with a categorical statement, "the manned aircraft will disappear by 1972 and with it the need for the Royal Air Force as a separate strategic arm. The main role of aircraft will be to provide fire power in support of the ground forces". This is the sort of unmitigated humbug the RAF had to contend with from the Army in the 1930s, and had it prevailed Britain would have lost the war in 1940.

The attacks on the deterrent, Bomber Command and the Royal Air Force continued with undiminished fury and undisguised antagonism up to the time of the general election when, with the advantage of apparently complete freedom of the air on sound and vision, the hymn of hate was droned out with nauseating regularity in the sure and certain knowledge that the Services could not retaliate. The RAF had no redress whatever misrepresentation was indulged in, and it was apparent that no other source of information was to be invited to give a contrary view on a vexed and complex subject, which so few people appeared to understand. The RAF Public Relations branch in the

THE ANTI-NUCLEAR CAMPAIGN

Ministry was at an all-time low and it was not until after the election
that the real purpose behind the degrading campaign was exposed.
Labour's election plank was rooted in Wilson's promises to
"renegotiate" the Nassau Agreement, get rid of nuclear weapons and
probably the RAF as well. He succeeded in silencing the raucous
voices of CND and pacifying his left-wing and other irrational
supporters by promises he could not keep.

The episode was not without its funny side, of course. The *Daily
Telegraph* revealed in November 1964, that the defence correspondent
of *The Times* had not only formulated the Labour Party's defence
policy for the election, but, unknown to them, he had also been the
architect of the Liberal defence manifesto – an equally futile
document. Soon after the election, the defence correspondent of *The
Times*, Mr Gwynn-Jones, was made Minister of *Dis*armament in the
Wilson government, and elevated to the peerage as Lord Chalfont. In
office, Wilson failed to fulfil the promises made to the left-wing of his
party on the renegotiation of the Nassau Agreement or the abolition of
nuclear weapons. The infamous cliché that the British independent
nuclear deterrent was "not British, not independent, and not a
deterrent", attributed to Gwynn-Jones and used by Wilson and his
Labour supporters throughout the election campaign, was quickly
dropped, and even the antics of the "Ban-the-Bomb" movement
became less ridiculous until they faded from the scene altogether,
having achieved nothing.

The year 1964 was notable for a number of other unfortunate
incidents, not least the end of the Valiants after long and reliable
service in the V-bomber force. Metal fatigue was discovered in one of
the aircraft after a normal training flight which might have had serious
repercussions but for the skill of the crew. After a thorough inspection
of all Valiants, it was decided not to spend money on a repair scheme
but to scrap them all. This meant a serious reduction in our
contribution to SACEUR and to the strike capability of Bomber
Command in the nuclear and conventional roles. But the loss was
offset to some extent by the prospect of the introduction of a new and
highly sophisticated tactical strike and reconnaissance aircraft, the
TSR-2. Development of the aircraft was well advanced; it was ahead
of any other multi-role aircraft anywhere in the world, including the

United States, and it was already known that it would have a nuclear capability at ranges sufficient to enable strikes to be made against targets in the Soviet Union. But sinister forces were again at work in Westminster and Whitehall, and another saga similar to that which surrounded Skybolt was about to unfold.

By the end of 1964, the shrill trumpets of the political propagandists were muted, the laurels had been handed out, and a measure of sanity returned to discussions on military affairs, which the events of the previous three months had thrown into disarray. Neither the capability of Bomber Command nor the validity of the British independent nuclear deterrent had changed in the slightest during this period. Bomber Command's capability and its contribution to British and allied defence requirements over the whole field of nuclear and conventional strategy was unimpaired and would remain so, until the responsibility for Britain's future nuclear force was taken over by the Navy in four or five years time.

The enormous potential nuclear striking power which Bomber Command possessed in 1962-63 when, in addition to the V-bomber force, it also operated the Thor intermediate-range ballistic missile force, was surpassed only by the United States. The ability of the Command to deliver accurately hundreds of megatons to targets anywhere within a radius of 1,500-2,500 miles from bases in the United Kingdom, Near East, Middle East or Far East, was indeed formidable. After 1963, however, there were unfortunate decisions not motivated by defence needs, which were bound to affect the weight of nuclear destruction which could be despatched in a retaliatory attack; but not the ability of the Command to deliver its attacks accurately and swiftly.

The introduction of Polaris submarines in 1968, whose capability was confined solely to the nuclear strike role in war, could not replace the V-bomber force in the nuclear deterrent or nuclear strike role and Polaris submarines had no capability in conventional war. If at least seven submarines had been produced, and Britain had maintained its V-bomber force, its claim to possession of a credible strategic nuclear deterrent force might have been preserved, but defence requirements, not for the first time, were subordinated to political expediency.

11

Labour Slashes Defence

Flushed with his election victory, Wilson lost no time in seeking an invitation to Washington. Not unnaturally, the electorate expected him to fulfil his pledge to the left-wing of his party to "renegotiate the Nassau Agreement and the proposal to buy Polaris submarines from the United States". He did visit Washington, but admitted on his return that the Nassau Agreement had not even been discussed. To add insult to injury, Wilson not only accepted that Britain had an independent deterrent, which he had no intention of abolishing, he actually supported a new one – the Atlantic Nuclear Force (ANF) – in which other European countries would be invited to have a say in the direction and control of the nuclear force. But he was careful to retain control of the British force for purely national contingencies – an arrangement which had been introduced by Macmillan when he accepted the Polaris deal in 1962. The British nuclear force was, of course, already assigned to SACEUR in war. The Atlantic Nuclear Force, not surprisingly, was sunk.

It was in 1963 that another scheme, first proposed in 1961 by a United States professor, named Robert Bowie, who was a consultant to the United States State Department, began to assume political and military importance for the future of NATO out of all proportion to its likely effectiveness or military practicability. The plan became known as the Multilateral Nuclear Force (MLF), and envisaged a fleet of twenty-five surface vessels built to resemble normal merchant ships. Each ship was to be armed with eight Polaris missiles and manned by a mixed crew from at least three nations. The entire force was to be operated and controlled by the countries supporting the project, who would have the right of veto over its use. To military strategists in the armed forces on both sides of the Atlantic this preposterous concept was so naïve that it quickly earned the nickname of "Fred Karno's Navy".

It was estimated that the cost of the project would be in the region of £1,500 million over a ten-year period. The United States and Germany were to contribute 80 per cent of the cost, Britain about 10 per cent and the other NATO countries taking part in the scheme were to make up the rest. Britain took part in the initial discussions and the project even reached the stage where a ship was fitted out and manned for trials. It was not made clear which language would be adopted for the orderly conduct of operations (if a common language was decided upon), or where two or three thousand bilingual sailors could be recruited to man the fleet. If a common language was not acceptable, no one had worked out how many interpreters would be required to convey the captain's orders to the ship's company to ensure the safety of the vessel while at sea. What would be likely to happen in the event that the fleet became involved in a war was not apparently discussed. Apart from these minor difficulties, the vulnerability of surface ships disguised to look like merchant ships (which was nothing more than a crude copy of the 'Q' ships used in World War I) was positively frightening.

Discussions on this ludicrous plan were still taking place at the time of the general election in October 1964, even though the whole concept was doomed to failure. Commenting on the MLF, Denis Healey, Labour's Defence Minister, said "the ambiguity on the question of control could make the MLF a major factor for disintegrating the alliance ... it is easy to understand why the German Defence Minister has already given notice that his country will not long remain content with a situation in which, having paid 80 per cent of the European contribution towards the mixed manned fleet, Germany must accept not only an American veto on its use, but also the veto of the other European countries. In my opinion, Britain could play an important role in shifting the argument about the mixed manned fleet into more fruitful fields by offering to put all her own nuclear weapons without exception into such a multilateral force". Could confusion be more confounded. The whole scheme collapsed for lack of support or enthusiasm by the NATO countries, including

Britain, though Healey's suggestion was interesting in the light of future proposals and actions by the British Labour Government.

The French, of course, would have nothing to do with Atlantic Nuclear Forces or Multilateral Nuclear Forces. During the Skybolt fiasco in Nassau, de Gaulle was offered a similar deal to that accepted by Britain, but he rejected it, and the whole depressing episode contributed to de Gaulle's persistent veto of Britain's efforts to join the European Economic Community in the years that followed. He decided to go his own way and produce his own independent nuclear deterrent, entirely under French control, based on the triad concept of manned bombers, ground-launched ballistic missiles in hardened silos and submarine-launched ballistic missiles. With no assistance from any other power, his programme took longer than either the British or Russian, but it is today a respectable independent nuclear deterrent, far superior to Britain's four submarines, and it is solely under French control.

Although Wilson did not make any official policy pronouncement on the subject when his government was installed in Westminster, it was clear that he had accepted as a fact of life that Britain had an independent nuclear deterrent and that the majority of the British people wanted to keep it. However, it had to be recognized, that when the Polaris submarines took over, there would no longer be an independent nuclear deterrent, and many knowledgeable people questioned whether it was value for money. It had been intended to build a minimum of five submarines, but the Labour Government cancelled the fifth. But the die was cast, and from 1963 the Navy began the task of building up a submarine force of four submarines, armed with Polaris missiles supplied by the United States. They adopted a scheme similar to that pioneered by the RAF so successfully in introducing the American Thor missile force into Bomber Command in 1958. The submarines were to be built in British yards and equipped with nuclear reactor propulsion systems which required American assistance, but the nuclear warheads for the Polaris missiles were to be made in Britain. The RAF already had a plentiful supply of warheads of various kinds, both atomic and thermonuclear, and no difficulties were envisaged by the Atomic Weapons Research Establishment at Aldermaston in designing suitable warheads. It was forecast that the first submarine would be ready for service in about four years, meantime the British nuclear deterrent would continue to be the responsibility of RAF Bomber Command.

With the demise of Skybolt and the withdrawal from service of the Valiant force, the strength of Bomber Command had been considerably reduced. But the new TSR-2 strike and reconnaissance aircraft, approaching the flight test stage showed great promise. It was conceived in 1957, when the Conservative Government issued the famous Sandys Defence White Paper virtually sealing the fate of the strategic bomber and the supersonic fighter in favour of surface-to-surface missiles in the strategic nuclear role and surface-to-air missiles in the air defence role. The contents of this ill-conceived White Paper provided unlimited ammunition for the opponents of air power who had persistently demonstrated their ignorance of its role in modern war and how it could best be applied. But even they could not find an alternative means of conducting tactical reconnaissance or interdiction strikes on or near the battlefield. A missile was not yet capable of the powers of reasoning or deduction which was still the prerogative of a human pilot. The Army had acknowledged that this particular role of air power was vital to them in any future war. As a result of the Sandys strategy, the supersonic bomber (Avro 730) and the Swallow variable geometry aircraft designed as possible replacements for the V-bombers ten years ahead were cancelled.

Theorists in the United States had similar views on the future of manned aircraft. Fortunately the more enlightened and experienced air strategists in Strategic Air Command were able to make intelligent value judgements on the relative merits and roles of missiles and manned aircraft and were successful in convincing Congress that the manned aircraft was not obsolete. They have been proved right by subsequent events, while in Britain a collection of self-appointed experts, who turned out to be little better than cranks, imposed their crude ideas on members of Parliament totally incapable of understanding the new technological age that had dawned in the 1960s and in which Britain was playing a leading role.

Early in 1965, the Wilson Government, in pursuance of its policy of reducing defence expenditure, cancelled a number of other projects destined for the RAF, including the HS-681 jet transport and the Hawker P-1154 supersonic fighter, but not the TSR-2. It had successfully completed its first test flight on 27th September 1964, just before the election, and it appeared that its future was assured even under the destructive policies of a Labour Government. This turned out to be yet another sorry saga of ill-conceived defence policies, designed for the pacification of the left-wing of the Party rather than for the defence of the country.

The TSR-2 was intended to meet the needs of the RAF in the twin roles in the 1960s and beyond. Competitive tenders were invited from industry and a number of aircraft firms appeared eager to accept a new challenge in aircraft design and performance. But the aircraft industry had been thrown into a state of turmoil by the announcements contained in the 1957 Defence White Paper and by the Government's decision to launch a massive programme designed to reorganize and streamline the aircraft and aero-engine industries. The reason given was that future orders for military aircraft would be insufficient to sustain the large number of independent companies then engaged in aeronautical engineering. The upshot of the Government's proposals was the amalgamation of the Bristol Aeroplane Company, English Electric and Vickers, to form the British Aircraft Corporation, which became the organization responsible for the design, production and flight test programme to meet the requirements of Air Staff policy under OR-343, later designated TSR-2.

The specification required the aircraft to operate at a height of 200 feet above ground level with automatic, terrain-following radar, at speeds up to Mach 1.1, and at high altitude of up to Mach 2. It was to be capable of a radius of action of 1,000-1,500 nautical miles and a ferry range of 3,000 nautical miles. Its roles were stated to be photographic and radar reconnaissance and strike operations with conventional and nuclear weapons. It was to be capable of operating from semi-prepared surfaces in all weathers, day or night, with the minimum of ground support. To meet these tasks, the TSR-2 was to be equipped with fully automatic flight control, navigation and attack systems of very advanced design, terrain-following radar, and have inherent long structural fatigue life to meet the exacting conditions of high-speed, low-level operations over long distances.

The Air Staff in formulating these demanding requirements were well aware of developments in air defence, especially in the Soviet Union. This would reach fruition in the decade when the new aircraft would be developed and deployed operationally, even though it was two years before Gary Powers was shot down by Soviet surface-to-air missiles. While the RAF were specifying requirements for the TSR-2, the Navy were also acquiring a new carrier borne strike aircraft. They had already signed contracts with the Blackburn Aircraft Company to produce the NA-39, later named the Buccaneer. But the cost of aircraft carriers was escalating at an alarming rate and their utility in a future war was seriously questioned by people in the Defence Ministry, including sailors, as well as by others outside. CVA 01, the last proposal by the Navy for a carrier of conventional design, was so costly that in combination with the Polaris force it would have vastly increased the Navy's share of the defence budget at the expense of the other two Services. Not even Mountbatten's dominant influence could have prevailed within the Chiefs-of-Staff Committee to the extent that the Army and RAF could meekly acquiesce to such demands.

It was at this stage that the Navy proposed a common strike aircraft for the Fleet Air Arm and the RAF, and, of course, the Buccaneer was suggested. The Air Staff rightly rejected a proposal which could not possibly meet the RAF's requirements. The Buccaneer was designed to operate from carriers at sea, where enemy defences were likely to be considerably less than the opposition to be encountered over enemy territory in attacks against important targets already known to be heavily defended. The Navy believed that by involving the RAF in the development of the Buccaneer and subsequently buying it, they could reduce the costs of a new carrier and its aircraft to the extent that they could put forward more persuasive arguments in favour of the carrier task force concept dear to Mountbatten's heart, but not universally acceptable to the Navy. It was a highly controversial debate while it lasted and had it succeeded Britain would have been saddled with costly aircraft carriers, as well as a submarine force of questionable military value.

Meanwhile TSR-2 project progressed under the British Aircraft Corporation throughout the early 1960s, but with the inevitable problems that accompany any new aeronautical project incorporating design features and performance characteristics at the frontiers of science, not previously encountered by any other country. Delays occurred because of teething troubles within the new industrial re-organization and Air Staff specification changes, but by September 1964 the prototype was ready for test flying. The general election was only a month away and already Labour politicians, aided and abetted by sections of the Press, were sniping at what they regarded as an expensive and unnecessary aircraft. Trouble with the Olympus engines imposed restrictions on the duration and scope of the first flight on 27th September, but despite this problem the initial test was a success within the limitations imposed. Further problems before the second flight encouraged an anti-TSR-2 lobby to step up their campaign. In the first three months of 1965 twenty flights were completed, including high speed low-level runs and supersonic flight, during which the aircraft met the specifications required by the Air Staff.

Pressure from the left-wing of the Labour Party and the Government's determination to reduce defence expenditure, put the TSR-2 on the list of possible candidates for cancellation early in March 1965. It was about this time that people woke up to the fact that the aircraft had a performance enabling operation in the nuclear strategic role as well as in tactical strike and reconnaissance. This infuriated the lobbies and gave Healey additional grounds for considering abandoning the whole project. On 6th April 1965, suddenly and with no coherent explanation, orders were issued to stop work on the TSR-2 and to destroy all aircraft and the jigs and tools used in their construction. Then followed the biggest act of government sponsored vandalism ever witnessed in this country. Attempts were made to erase the TSR-2 by axe and saw in an orgy of destruction that sickened even the workmen who had to execute Healey's orders.

As a palliative to the Chief of the Air Staff, Healey announced that the Government had decided to purchase the American F-111, then undergoing trials and which Healey claimed would meet all the Air Staff requirements and would be much cheaper than the TSR-2. Zuckerman had always favoured buying American equipment and his influence was discernible in Mountbatten's hostility to the TSR-2. Mountbatten was dedicated to ensuring the Navy's survival, if necessary at the expense of the RAF, through the aircraft carrier and its associated escort vessels. The TSR-2 was an obstacle to the achievement of his ambition, following the RAF's initial rejection of the Buccaneer, and it had to be removed. Healey it would appear had no intention of buying the F-111 for the RAF, and as soon as Mountbatten left the Ministry of Defence, he lost no time in cancelling the aircraft carrier programme as well.

A general review of British strategy was initiated soon after Labour took office in 1965, the object being to see what reductions in defence expenditure could be achieved to pacify the left-wing without upsetting the trade unions whose members would lose their jobs. Defence of the Realm was not a primary consideration. The Socialists had long since resolved that Britain should liquidate her commitments overseas, and after futile exercises in such dubious strategies as the "Island Strategy", in which it was proposed to develop a chain of islands between Britain and Singapore to act as staging posts for transport aircraft flying troops out to reinforce skeleton garrisons in the Far East, the 1966 Defence Review was published. It revealed the Labour Government's decision to cut drastically the defence budget and overseas commitments in the decade ahead and in the process to reduce the strength of the Armed Forces by half.

While all this was going on, the RAF had lost the TSR-2 through the combined efforts of Labour politicians, sections of the Press, and the powerful Navy lobby. They had succeeded in denying the RAF the only major operational aircraft replacement for the 1960s and beyond. The TSR-2's strategic nuclear capability would have made a valuable contribution to Britain's miniature nuclear force of four Polaris submarines, but even this important aspect of nuclear deterrence was ignored. In a Press interview, as reported in *The Times*, Mountbatten is said to have told a conference in Australia in March 1965, just before the TSR-2 was cancelled, that Britain did not have an independent nuclear deterrent. Angry at this grossly improper statement by a Chief of Defence Staff, the Opposition raised the matter in the House of Commons Defence Debate on 4th March 1965. In reply, Healey said: "The reason why members of the opposition front bench and the Leader of the Opposition have dropped all this talk about an independent nuclear deterrent is that the

Rt Hon Gentleman knows that it does not exist and has never existed. He knows the Chief of Defence Staff was talking the truth when he said at a Press Conference in Australia that Britain does not have an independent nuclear deterrent". If, of course, he was referring to the acquisition of Polaris submarines by the Navy, then he was correct; Britain would not have an independent nuclear deterrent. But that was four years away and Bomber Command of the RAF was still the British independent nuclear deterrent. Mountbatten probably knew before he left for Australia that the TSR-2 was going to be cancelled and he also knew that the Royal Australian Air Force was interested in buying it, but they mysteriously switched their interest to the American F-111 even after a visit to Britain, seeing the aircraft and confirming to the RAF that the TSR-2 would meet all their requirements. Someone must surely have told them that the TSR-2 was going to be cancelled well before the official announcement was made by Healey.

An interesting comment on the TSR-2 affair was provided by Air Chief Marshal Sir Claude Pelly, Controller of Aircraft, Ministry of Supply 1957-1959. Writing in a well-known military journal some time after the event, Sir Claude took to task its editor, a retired naval officer, for writing a scurrilous editorial on the TSR-2 which misrepresented facts and was typical of the attitude of the naval lobby at that time. Sir Claude recalled the requirements of OR-343 and emphasized the importance of low-level capability in the strike and reconnaissance roles. He pointed out that the operational requirements as laid down by the Air Staff called for a completely new structural design which no variant of the Buccaneer could fulfil. He also observed that the word 'bomber' was out of fashion in Whitehall and that Sandys had himself selected the title "Tactical-Strike-Reconnaissance" aircraft for the TSR-2.

Sir Claude Pelly concluded his strictures on the editor of the journal with the observation that he found some of the statements in the editorial more than merely misleading and the notion that what had been saved by cancelling the TSR-2 should automatically be devoted to building more aircraft carriers a somewhat facile deduction.

By the time the 1967 Defence White Paper was published, detailing Britain's proposals for abandoning all her overseas commitments and concentrating her defence effort on Europe, the first of the Polaris submarines was about to enter service and the time was approaching when responsibility for Britain's strategic nuclear force would be handed over to the Navy. It is significant that at this stage the anti-RAF lobbies, both in and out of Parliament, who had been so antagonistic to Bomber Command and the British independent nuclear deterrent, and who had persistently claimed that it was not British, not independent, and not a deterrent, referred to the Polaris force as the "British nuclear deterrent". The word "independent" was dropped, but the nuclear deterrent had apparently become respectable and credible and even British under naval direction, when everyone knew that the missiles were American. The paradox continues to this day.

Four submarines which could only guarantee one on station at any given time is hardly a deterrent, certainly not to the Soviet Union, and the Polaris force is today assigned to SACEUR simply as "a contribution to the West's nuclear deterrent forces", the vast majority of which are American. Britain will never again possess a military force with the power to deter or destroy which Bomber Command of the Royal Air Force represented from 1957 to 1968. In 1968, the remnants of a once great command were incorporated in a new organization, called Strike Command, and Bomber Command was abolished. The remaining Vulcan aircraft were assigned to SACEUR in a tactical role and the Victors were converted to tankers. They retained their nuclear weapons and could, in theory, be used in a strategic role, but their chances of penetrating enemy defences are slim, and as they are more than twenty years old, it is time they were retired.

When Bomber Command finally handed over to the Navy in 1968, there was little ceremony, out of deference to the susceptibilities of the left-wing of the Labour Party. There was not even a letter of thanks or appreciation to the men and women whose devoted service over a decade had provided Britain with a truly independent nuclear deterrent, which brought her prestige and influence she could not otherwise have enjoyed and which has long since diminished, even within the European alliance and the Economic Community.

In the statement on defence estimates 1966, it had been announced that in order to reduce defence expenditure, further reductions in overseas commitments and in the strength of the Armed Forces would be necessary. This meant a drastic revision of British defence policy and strategy summarized in the statement that "Britain would not again undertake major operations of war, except in co-operation with allies and would make commitments to friends and allies dependent on the provision in time of whatever facilities were needed on the spot". The ambiguities of this announcement were apparent to any military strategist, but a supplementary statement on defence policy in 1967 spelled out Labour's new role for Britain in world affairs and her future strategy. It detailed revised proposals for the deployment of British forces including withdrawal from the Mediterranean, Middle East, and Far East. The Aden base was to be evacuated in 1968 and deployments in Malaysia and Singapore were to be reduced by half in 1970. Commitments to the South-East Asia Treaty Organisation (SEATO) were to be honoured, but the forces declared to the alliance were to be reduced and the terms of the commitment altered. It was claimed that obligations to allies and the discharge of responsibility to Britain's remaining colonies could be accomplished by despatching forces from the United Kingdom rather than by basing them permanently overseas and to this end "new aircraft will enable us to move forces across the world faster and in larger numbers than was possible even a few years ago". All this was but a prelude to a much more drastic revision of defence policy only a year later.

The 1968 Defence White Paper announced that the Government had carried out a searching review of the whole range of public expenditure as one of the measures necessary for a radical solution to the country's balance of payments problems. A now familiar and boring theme. The major decisions affecting defence policy can be summarized broadly as follows:

(a) Britain's defence effort will in future be concentrated mainly in Europe and the North Atlantic area.

(b) We shall accelerate the withdrawal of our forces from Malaysia and Singapore, and complete it by the end of 1971. We shall also withdraw from the Persian Gulf by the same date.

(c) Service manpower will eventually be reduced by more than the

      75,000 forecast in the Supplementary Statement on Defence Policy 1967 (Cmnd 3357) and the reduction will be spread over a shorter time.

(*d*) The carrier force will be phased out as soon as the withdrawals from Malaysia, Singapore and the Persian Gulf have been completed and the rate of some new naval construction will be reduced.

(*e*) The Brigade of Gurkhas will be run down to 6,000 by 1971.

(*f*) The order for 50 F-111 aircraft has been cancelled and the Royal Air Force transport force will be cut.

(*g*) Support facilities including Headquarters and the Ministry of Defence will be cut.

(*h*) No special capability for use outside Europe will be maintained when our withdrawal from Singapore and Malaysia and the Persian Gulf is complete.

(*i*) We shall, however, retain a general capability based in Europe including the United Kingdom, which can be deployed overseas as, in our judgement, circumstances demand, and can support United Nations operations as necessary.

It was not necessary to add that these changes meant drastic revision of the role, size and shape of the Forces, their equipment and support. Since there was no replacement for the V-bombers, the RAF was compelled to abandon its ability to conduct long-range air operations in either the nuclear or conventional role. The Royal Air Force had, in effect, ceased to have the ability to apply independent air power in war which had been a key element in the concept of air power and air strategy since operations in the third dimension — the air — became possible in World War I. The TSR-2 and the F-111 had been cancelled; both had long-range strike and reconnaissance capability with or without in-flight refuelling, but the 1968 White Paper made it clear that the future roles of the RAF would be confined to air defence, ground attack and fighter/tactical reconnaissance mainly in Europe. Since no British aircraft were to be available, the Government announced that it would acquire some Phantom aircraft from the United States. They had been in operation with the United States Air Force and Navy for years.

As events have unfolded over the last decade, the decision to cancel the TSR-2 has been shown to be an unmitigated disaster for which the Labour Government under Harold Wilson must accept full responsibility. Less than two years later, it became necessary to enter into a collaborative venture with Germany and Italy to provide a strike/reconnaissance aircraft for the RAF, capable of low-level operations against deep penetration targets with nuclear or conventional weapons. The roles of the aircraft as listed in the specification were similar to those for the TSR-2. In 1980, some ten years after the project was launched, the MRCA (Multi Role Combat Aircraft), now named Tornado, will enter operational service with the RAF. More than 200 for the strike/reconnaissance role are on order at a cost of nearly £8 million per aircraft. If the TSR-2 had not been cancelled, it would have been five years ahead of its time and even American forces might have been compelled to buy it. It might even have become the standard strike aircraft for all NATO forces and would have been a great deal cheaper than the Tornado. But British Labour politicians and those who support them have an unhappy knack of sabotaging most of Britain's advanced technology developments, when they do not actually present them to the Communists as they did with the Nene and Derwent jet engines in 1946.

For the past ten years the Navy has operated with efficiency and dedication four Polaris submarines as Britain's contribution to the West's nuclear deterrent and nuclear strategic strike forces, most of which, as has been said, are American. But the submarines were designed for a life cycle of 20-25 years and, given the lead-time required to produce a replacement, decisions on the future of Britain's nuclear force must be taken within the next year or, at most, two years. The last Labour Government gave no indication that it would replace the Polaris force; on the contrary, some of its spokesmen implied that if they won the next election the Polaris force would not be replaced. Given Labour's record of deception and reversals in defence policy, it is nevertheless likely that they might support a follow-on nuclear force. The Conservative Party, of course, has long been committed to maintaining a British nuclear force and within a year must decide what form it should take.

12

End of Bomber Command

Now that the dust has settled, past errors in defence policy have been exposed and those responsible for the depressing state of British defence policy in general and nuclear policy in particular have been exposed. Before looking to what may be a bleak future, it is appropriate to record briefly just how important the manned bomber was to the nuclear deterrent posture of the 'sixties and the important role it still plays in modern concepts of nuclear deterrence and nuclear strike capability. The appalling error made by Duncan Sandys, the Conservative Defence Minister in 1957, when he claimed that missiles would replace manned aircraft within a decade in the offensive and defensive uses of air power, was not shared by either the United States or the Soviet Union. It is all the more regrettable that the statement was made just as the V-bombers were entering operational service with Bomber Command and were acknowledged to be far superior to anything the Russians could produce. They were the envy of Strategic Air Command of the United States Air Force as well. Today, two decades later, new and more sophisticated manned aircraft are being introduced into the inventories of all modern air forces throughout the world.

It is essential to an understanding of the strength and effectiveness of Bomber Command during the 1957-67 decade, to know at least something of the roles of the Command, its equipment, control and communications systems, alert and readiness plans and how the force operated. The threat to these islands and the defence which it was possible to mount against that threat, induced the statement in the 1957 Defence White Paper that "Britain must possess an element of nuclear deterrent power of her own". Since 1959, the Soviet Union has steadily deployed a menacing and growing force of intermediate-range ballistic missiles, especially the current SS-20, and manned aircraft capable of delivering large numbers of nuclear weapons up to megaton yield against a wide variety of targets. The missiles could be launched from ground installations, from submarines or from aircraft, and no matter what view was taken of the situation, the fact remained that there was virtually no defence against the missile threat and only a limited one against manned aircraft.

The new roles of Bomber Command were detailed in the Commander-in-Chief's Directive issued in 1963. The first one stated that the Command was to act as the principal national deterrent to general war. This was its peace role and it did not change throughout the life of the Command. If the deterrent philosophy failed and general nuclear war broke out, Bomber Command's second role was to destroy those targets assigned to it by SACEUR in accordance with his nuclear strike plan. This was a modification to the original directive and reflected the assignment of the whole of the V-bomber force to SACEUR following the Nassau Agreement. The third role charged Bomber Command with the task of reinforcing overseas commands as required. Such was the flexibility and adaptability of the V-bombers that this role could readily be assumed in either limited conventional or nuclear war.

Bomber Command consisted of three distinct forces. The V-bomber force equipped with Vulcan and Victor Mk 2, was entirely under national control but assigned to SACEUR in war. The reconnaissance force, armed with Victor Mk 2s and Canberras, was also under national control and operated by Bomber Command on behalf of all three Services and many civil authorities in peace; in war it was assigned to SACEUR. The tanker force, entirely under national control, had no specific war tasks. It was operated by Bomber Command to provide in-flight refuelling facilities for all RAF Commands and the Royal Navy as and when required.

The terms of assignment to SACEUR, effective from 23rd May 1963, placed Bomber Command under SACEUR on the outbreak of war. In peace, direct planning with SHAPE was exercised for targeting, co-ordination of nuclear strikes and the execution of those strikes in so far as they affected SACEUR's strike plan.

160

Organizational functions in peacetime, such as states of readiness, deployment and dispersal, logistics and support – which cover such things as the type of aircraft, weapons, training of crews and types of equipment – remained under national control. Aircraft could be withdrawn from SACEUR at any time for use in purely national interests.

To support the front line, there was a large training organization including the Bombing School, the Operational Conversion Units (where crews trained to operate V-bombers) and a nuclear weapons school, where nuclear theory and practice was taught, including the types of nuclear weapons with which the Command was equipped. These ranged from small kiloton to megaton yield weapons. At the other end of the scale, V-bombers were capable of carrying large quantities of conventional high explosive bombs. Included in the nuclear armoury was the Blue Steel stand-off missile, with a megaton warhead. At all the training schools and in the operational squadrons, great emphasis was placed on the importance of bombing accuracy. In practice-bombing sorties, crews endeavoured to improve their capability in competition among themselves and in friendly rivalry with Strategic Air Command. To emphasize the importance of accuracy, it is useful to relate bombing error to radii of destruction of nuclear weapons. In war, an allowance for unassessable factors must always be added to peacetime bombing results, but even taking a pessimistic view of the average crew's ability to bomb under the stresses of enemy action, it would still be possible to achieve the annihilation of a city the size of Liverpool with a single one-megaton weapon.

Weapons and the means of delivering them were, however, only part of the problem. A continuous study of the difficulties of penetrating enemy air space in the face of changing and improving defences was necessary to meet a constant demand for improvements in equipment and tactics. The impact of computers, systems analysis and cost-effectiveness studies was felt in this country just as much as in the United States, and highly refined analytical techniques were used to determine the chances of bombers penetrating enemy defence, so that the weight of effort required to achieve a given level of destruction on a selected target or target system could be calculated.

On the results of these intricate studies, some taking weeks to determine, it was possible to assess the effectiveness of the force. It is all the more remarkable, therefore, that some self-styled experts claimed to be able to reach different conclusions, without the benefit of detailed knowledge of any of the factors involved and with little or no idea of the workings of a computer.

Factors to be taken into account in these calculations were the performance of the aircraft, bombing ability and the effectiveness of the weapons; whether evasive routing was possible, and the choice between high and low-level flight patterns, or a combination of both; the degree of effectiveness of electronic countermeasures equipment; the effects of other and possibly earlier nuclear strikes on enemy defences; and the advantage which a stand-off missile might confer on the attacker, and how best to exploit it. Taking these factors individually, it can be seen that in the performance of its aircraft, Bomber Command had a force second to none in the world. At high-level the V-bombers were superior to any aircraft operating in a comparable role except the American B-58 Hustler. At low-level there was no aircraft in service anywhere with a better performance against deep penetration targets. Low-level became the standard mode of operation in Bomber Command after the cancellation of Skybolt, and would have enabled the V-force to penetrate enemy radars virtually unseen. Most of the complex radar systems deployed throughout the world at that time were designed for use against high-level attack and the majority of the equipments had little or no capability below 1,000 feet. To produce and deploy a completely new system with comparable performance against aircraft flying at heights of 200 feet and below was to prove both difficult and time consuming. A new generation of aircraft, then under development, took advantage of this shortcoming in defence systems and despite spectacular claims to the contrary there was no effective low-level missile defence system deployed anywhere in the world for a further five years. Even today, low-level air defence is less than 50 per cent effective.

This deficiency in defence systems was an important factor in the bomber's favour, provided the right route was chosen in approaching the target and it was not difficult to take full advantage of it along the lengthy frontiers the Russians had to defend. The nonsense talked by certain commentators about the V-bombers not being able to penetrate Soviet defences was born either of gross ignorance or a desire deliberately to misrepresent the truth. Probably a little of both.

Electronic countermeasures play an important part in a bomber force's ability to penetrate defences in both nuclear and conventional war, and a great deal of research was carried out into ways of degrading a defence system. The V-bombers were equipped with a comprehensive and effective array of countermeasures equipment and the search for improvements in design and performance was unending. The missile age did not reduce requirements in this field, it increased them. The stand-off missile, Blue Steel, was immune from attack by manned aircraft or surface-to-air missiles for most of its life but the RAF was well aware that this situation could not be expected to last indefinitely, though they were confident that it would prevail for many years. In the meantime, new devices could be invented to keep abreast of enemy developments in the defence field. Both the Vulcans and Victors could carry Blue Steel and in the low-level role they constituted a fully viable and effective nuclear strike force.

It will be remembered that the 1958 Defence White Paper stipulated "if the deterrent is to be effective, it must not be thought capable of being knocked out on the ground". It was this statement that gave authority for the development of the well-known Bomber Command alert and readiness plan which, when fully implemented, was the finest in the world and the envy of all. Three things are essential for an effective readiness organization: a warning system, a variable and flexible readiness state and a dispersal plan. Warning comes in two main categories, strategic and tactical. Strategic warning is a continuous process and is made up from intelligence received from many sources, so that from day to day a pattern is traced giving the likely trend of events and indicating when the political climate is about to blow hot or cold. From such warning there is ample time to alert a bomber force or change its readiness state. Tactical warning, on the other hand, gives information of the imminence of attack from either manned aircraft or missiles. Time is at a premium and tactical warning was the condition around which the whole of the Bomber Command alert system was designed.

The manned aircraft threat from the East was covered by NATO and Fighter Command radars, information from which was fed directly to the Bomber Command operations centre. The manned aircraft threat to the North American continent was covered by a network of radars called the DEW line, whose headquarters was at Colorado Springs, the nerve centre of the whole North American Air Defence Organization, NORAD. Information available from the DEW line radars was also fed into the operations centre at Bomber Command, so that there was continuous and up-to-date intelligence of activity over practically the whole northern hemisphere. Any manned aircraft threat to the United Kingdom provided at least two hours warning of approach, which was more than enough to alter the readiness state of the V-bombers, but warning of a missile threat was very much less and it was this threat that most concerned Bomber Command.

The Ballistic Missile Early Warning System explained in Chapter 8 is still in operation. Thus, there was full cover of any missile threat likely to be launched against Europe or North America. The Americans would get fifteen-minutes warning of an intercontinental missile attack and Europe, including Britain, would get about eight minutes warning of an intermediate-range missile attack, assuming the missiles were fired from Russian bases. If the firing sites were moved forward into the satellite countries the warning time would be cut to as little as four minutes and it was to this lower figure that the V-bomber force planned to react. From a tactical point of view it was considered that the Russians would be unlikely to attack Britain or Europe first, giving the United States clear warning that World War III had started. Simultaneous strikes on the two continents was more probable and this would give Britain the same warning time as America – fifteen minutes. The bomber force alert and readiness plan was therefore designed to achieve a four-minute reaction time and alert states ranged from 1 to 4.

Alert condition 4 was the normal state in which only a small proportion of the force was at fifteen-minutes readiness. The rest were free to carry out routine training including flights to overseas bases. The alert aircraft however, were armed with nuclear weapons and the crews briefed and ready for take-off if an emergency or crisis developed. Throughout the twenty-four hours they practised changing alert states up to and including engine starts. The next highest alert state, referred to as alert condition 3, could be ordered by the Commander-in-Chief at any time and was a precautionary condition involving preliminary preparations for arming all the V-bombers with nuclear weapons. Leave for personnel was stopped and other activities curtailed so that all available manpower and resources could be concentrated on the task of meeting the next highest state, alert condition 2. This called for full generation of all available V-bombers. Aircraft would be armed with nuclear weapons and crews briefed for their war missions. While this was in progress, alert condition 1 could be ordered if the Commander-in-Chief felt it would be wise to disperse the force, either for practice or to meet any emergency that might arise.

When dispersed, the force scattered to airfields throughout the British Isles, not more than four aircraft to each airfield and in some cases only two. These dispersal airfields had all the facilities needed to enable crews to remain at fifteen minutes readiness for take-off night and day for at least thirty days. The aircraft were parked on special operational readiness platforms, with direct communications from Bomber Command operations centre and from alternative control centres into the crew's living quarters and into the cockpits of the aircraft. All aircraft were modified to enable all four engines to be started simultaneously and external connections were pulled out automatically when the aircraft began to move forward prior to take-off.

Thus, if a scramble had been ordered there would have been a minimum of delay in launching the force. The best take-off time for four aircraft from the order to scramble was about two minutes thirty seconds under operational conditions but for demonstration purposes times as low as seventy seconds had been achieved. This means that the V-bomber force could have been off the ground well before the first strike of a ballistic missile attack. Once in the air, the force was under positive control, and would not have proceeded beyond a specified point without explicit instructions to do so. If no instructions were received by the crews for whatever reasons, they would automatically return to base. Every instruction had to be received and authenticated, checked inside the aircraft and acknowledged, so that

165

there could be no possibility of a mistake or misunderstanding. Since certain actions involving more than one member of the crew had to be completed before a nuclear weapon could be dropped live, the chances of accidental release, or deliberate unauthorized release by a member of the crew, were extremely remote. Dr Strangelove was a fantasy that played on the emotions and imagination of the more irrational and unstable elements of society. The events portrayed in that film have little resemblance to reality, but the authors of it made a fortune while at the same time, advancing the cause of nuclear disarmament which the Soviet Union appreciated.

It will be obvious that the communications organization necessary to achieve such quick reaction and control was both expensive and elaborate. Everything had to be duplicated and in certain cases quadruplicated, to be certain that faults in equipment, breakdown, enemy action or sabotage could not prevent orders reaching the crews by one of several means of communication. There were alternative control centres, and, as a final safeguard, an airborne control post was scrambled with the bomber aircraft to provide communications with the ground, with all bomber aircraft in the air, with a similar airborne control aircraft serving SACEUR and, finally, with SAC's airborne control aircraft. This elaborate and highly efficient system provided the means to communicate with control centres in the United Kingdom, on the continent of Europe and in America, either by radio or telephone from the ground, or by radio from the air, at all hours of the day or night, in any circumstances.

If, by some dread mischance the deterrent had failed and Bomber Command had received orders to attack targets in the Soviet Union, let there be no doubt or misunderstanding about the ability of the crews to carry out the missions assigned to them. They were capable of destroying most of the major cities in the Soviet Union. This was neither a boast nor sabre rattling; it was a simple fact of life which only the enemies of the Royal Air Force and the friends of the Soviet Union dispute. They were few in number but highly vocal and, like the empty kettle, made the most noise.

But nuclear strikes in general or global war were only one facet of Bomber Command's capability. It had tasks in peacetime which no other force could undertake and had to fulfil the additional roles while still maintaining its nuclear deterrent capability. Suitable bases for operation of V-bombers existed in Europe, Near East, Middle East, Far East and in Australia. All V-bombers could carry large loads of conventional bombs over great distances, and all were capable of being in-flight refuelled, so that their deployment to overseas bases was rapid; fifteen hours to Singapore and seven to Aden. They could be deployed with equal ease in either the conventional or nuclear mode and facilities existed for the storage and handling of nuclear weapons at overseas bases, so that they were a potent addition to the air strike capability of any overseas Commander-in-Chief.

The ground and air crews who maintained and flew the V-bombers were an élite corps, who carried out an exacting task, ready for action day and night, round the clock, year after year. Such a high state of readiness called for the highest standards of professional ability and for a sense of mission. Bomber Command crews had no illusions about the importance of the part they played in maintaining Britain's independent nuclear deterrent and providing a contribution to the West's overall military capability. They were very conscious of the responsibilities entrusted to them and of the fact that upon their efforts and efficiency depended the effectiveness of the force which was the main pillar of this country's defence policy for more than a decade. They were men of the highest calibre and their training requirements were strict and demanding, often involving long overseas detachments, away from their families. To men so dedicated to their task the attacks made upon Bomber Command, the Royal Air Force and the ability of the crews themselves, were all the more despicable. But they were not distracted from the all-important duty assigned to them. Instead, they quietly treated the tirades against Bomber Command and the nuclear deterrent with the contempt they deserved and in this they were joined by the vast majority of intelligent and rational people in this country.

Bomber Command, as Britain's nuclear deterrent, represented a capital investment of about £1,000 million. It had been Britain's deterrent force for a decade and at the start of its life represented 10 per cent of the total defence budget. In the 1966 defence budget of £2,120 millions, the deterrent took less than 4 per cent. Capital investment had come to an end and the force had been contracting, though it still had enormous assets in real estate in the form of the finest airfields and communications systems that modern engineering could devise, ready-made for any other type of aircraft that might be deployed in the deterrent and nuclear strike role. It had an excellent range of nuclear weapons and the finest aircrews in the world. Between 1965 and 1968, when the Command handed over the nuclear deterrent role to the Navy, the running costs of Bomber Command fell to an average of 2 per cent of the defence budget. No other force could have undertaken the tasks assigned to Bomber Command; certainly not submarines or aircraft carriers. It was one of the greatest blunders in recent military history when the RAF was deprived of its long-range strike capability in both the nuclear and conventional roles. The Americans, Russians and French have maintained bombers as part of their nuclear deterrent triad and nuclear strike forces. All three have credible independent nuclear deterrent forces. Britain has not.

Sir Winston Churchill put the choice before the British people simply and clearly when he said, "Sometimes in the past we have committed the folly of throwing away our arms. Under the mercy of providence and at great cost and sacrifice we have been able to recreate them when the need arose. But if we abandon our nuclear deterrent there will be no such second chance. To abandon it now would be to abandon it forever." The Labour Government did not heed those words of advice from the greatest Englishman to occupy the post of Prime Minister of this country for at least a century.

Britain is unlikely ever again to possess a force with the power to deter or to destroy which Bomber Command of the Royal Air Force represented between 1957 and 1968.

13

What of the Future?

There are only three truly credible, independent nuclear deterrents in the world today, those of the United States, the Soviet Union and France, though some would question the survivability of France's silo-based missiles and the penetration capability of her Mirage bombers. All three countries operate the triad system of surface-to-surface missiles in hardened silos, submarine-launched missiles, and strategic bombers. Each system has advantages and disadvantages, but between them they give a guarantee that a retaliatory response against any pre-emptive strike by a potential enemy would be swift and devastating – the essence of deterrence.

China is struggling manfully to achieve a credible nuclear deterrent capability, but so far she has managed to produce only medium and intermediate range missiles, with ranges of from 600 to 1,750 miles. A multi-stage ICBM, with a range of 3,000-3,5000 miles has been tested, but China is still a long way from producing an intercontinental capability comparable to that of the Soviet Union whom she sees as her implacable enemy. China also has a few heavy bombers, but neither they nor the IRBM's could reach important industrial targets in the western areas of the Soviet Union and it is questionable whether they could mount a successful counterforce attack on the Soviet missiles now ranged against Chinese nuclear and industrial targets. As far as is known, China has only one submarine fitted with launch tubes suitable for firing ballistic missiles, but the missiles are not yet available.

When Britain misguidedly abandoned surface-to-surface missiles by cancelling Blue Streak, and failed to acquire Skybolt or Minuteman from the United States, but accepted instead a small token force of four Polaris submarines (missiles supplied by the United States), she virtually opted out of the nuclear deterrent business altogether. With only one system, the Polaris submarines, the British force is dangerously exposed to a breakthrough in anti-submarine warfare (ASW) technology, to the deployment of new types of anti-ballistic missile defence (charged particle beams) and to sabotage or disruption of the cycle of carefully planned operations by Communist directed strikes, such as those which took place at British submarine yards in September 1978. A single strategic nuclear delivery system, whatever its merits at any particular time, is obviously less secure, less effective and less credible than a triad or even a dyad system. But if Britain cannot afford to have more than one delivery system, she must not opt out of the strategic nuclear business altogether – she must not become the first ex-nuclear power.

No military weapons system has yet been produced that could justify the description 'the ultimate weapon', which has sometimes in the past been accorded to the nuclear warhead. It is often not appreciated by the layman that the delivery system is far more important than the warhead, and in the application of modern technology to military weapons systems, the counter to the system under development is usually studied just as closely as the weapon itself, in both the design and development stages. Sir Robert Watson-Watt, the discoverer of radar, once said that to every measure sooner or later there is a countermeasure, and to every countermeasure there is a counter-countermeasure. Nuclear-powered submarines armed with ballistic missiles have enjoyed a degree of invulnerability from enemy attack while in the depths of the ocean not credited to other delivery systems, but sooner or later a counter to the submerged submarine or to the missiles it carries, or both, will be found; hence the constant search for new types of delivery systems that will survive for a time scale which would justify their development and production.

Britain's four Polaris submarines, *Resolution, Repulse, Renown* and *Revenge*, have been in service since 1968-70, and under current operating procedures it is possible to guarantee that there will always be one, and sometimes two, in position to fire ballistic missiles at targets in the Soviet Union within a range of 2,800 miles. This is provided that unforeseen events, such as damage or loss from collisions, or strikes at home ports, do not interrupt a scrupulously planned schedule, involving the rotation of the submarines between home port and operational area, routine maintenance and periodic overhauls. If the force were to be reduced to three submarines for any reason, it would not be possible to guarantee even one on station. A force of four such submarines is therefore the absolute minimum required to be sure of mounting a nuclear strike in the event of war.

The question whether one submarine, or even two, constitutes a strategic nuclear deterrent (independent or otherwise) to the Soviet Union has been the subject of debate since the Polaris submarines took over from RAF Bomber Command in 1968. If, as the Socialists and their supporters, sections of the media and the Navy lobby insisted, a force of all-British V-bombers, armed with British nuclear warheads and capable of delivering more than 200 megatons against more than 200 separate targets in the Soviet Union was not an independent nuclear deterrent, then by no stretch of the imagination can one or two submarines, capable of delivering nineteen megatons (at most) on thirty-two targets be considered a nuclear deterrent. In fact, since the Polaris force depends upon the United States for its missiles and support logistics it is not independent, and indeed is no longer referred to as a British nuclear deterrent, but as "an integral part of NATO's strategic nuclear force" (Statement on the Defence Estimates 1978). This being so, replacement of the existing force revolves around four main issues. First, whether it is necessary, desirable or possible to replace the existing force of four submarines. Secondly, if it is accepted that Britain should continue to make a contribution to NATO's strategic nuclear forces, what size should it be? Thirdly, what form should the replacement force take, bearing in mind that it will be ten years ahead before the new force is operational? Fourthly, how much would a replacement force cost — capital and running costs?

Strategic considerations, so far as Britain is concerned, are no longer relevant, since the force is to be simply a contribution to NATO and will, therefore, be targeted by NATO and come under the control of SACEUR, which means that it could only be used after authority for the use of nuclear weapons had been conveyed from the President of the United States to SACEUR. For Britain to insist on maintaining a degree of national control for use of the force in an extreme national emergency (as at present) really does not make much sense with a force which is palpably not an independent deterrent to the only likely enemy for as far ahead as can be foreseen. Who, other than the Soviet Union would be likely to threaten Britain or British interests to the extent that a nuclear strike would be justified? If it is considered that the Soviet Union might attack Britain in isolation, then, before doing so, it would not be beyond her capacity to neutralize the present force of four submarines. Each time a Polaris submarine leaves Faslane it is marked and shadowed by Soviet submarines, ships and aircraft, in the same way that NATO marks and shadows Soviet ships leaving their bases in the Kola peninsula. Submarines can be trailed by enemy submarines. Once out to sea and submerged it is much more difficult to locate and follow a nuclear submarine. But the Soviet Union is devoting large sums to research and development in anti-submarine technology, which could result in a breakthrough well within a decade – the time scale for developing another submarine force to replace Polaris.

The idea, popular a few years ago, that the possession of a strategic nuclear force by Britain, however small or incredible, might be used to 'trigger' the American force into retaliatory nuclear attacks on the Soviet Union in the event of a Soviet attack is not sustainable. The basis of the argument is that it would be difficult for the Soviets to detect the origin of a missile fired from a submerged submarine, and they would conclude that it came from a United States submarine. Since the Soviets achieved parity (and in some respects superiority) with the United States in strategic nuclear delivery systems, it is logical to assume that if a British missile were to be launched against the Soviet Union with the object of 'triggering' the United States strategic nuclear force, the Soviets would launch an assault on both continents simultaneously in the course of which Britain would probably be destroyed. The Soviets now have the capability to do this, where they did not have it only a few years ago.

Another fallacy which some politicians and military commentators cling to is that Britain's possession of a strategic nuclear force confers upon her privileges and prestige which are not accorded to other non-nuclear European countries. This was true in the late 'fifties and during the 'sixties, when Bomber Command represented Britain's independent nuclear deterrent, but it is no longer self-evident. The SALT negotiations are conducted entirely bilaterally between the Soviet Union and the United States, though NATO is informed of the progress of the negotiations and the likely outcome is discussed. The British Foreign Office has an *ad hoc* committee, which is supposed to study nuclear affairs as they affect arms control, but its impact on the United States SALT negotiating team or its posture is nil. Equally, any agreements entered into by the United States and the Soviet Union are signed and ratified by the two superpowers, whether Britain or any other NATO country approves or not.

If Britain decided to maintain an independent strategic nuclear deterrent against the Soviet Union, it would have to be a force that was credible; one that could not be destroyed in a pre-emptive attack or rendered inoperable by other means. It would have to have the ability in a second strike to penetrate Soviet defences and inflict unacceptable damage on Soviet towns and industrial complexes, and to destroy residual Soviet hard targets such as missile silos. The present force could not with certainty achieve any of these objectives and a much larger triad of delivery systems would be needed to guarantee that the Soviets would be deterred from attacking this country. It is true that the United States is currently examining the vulnerability of their Minuteman silo-based missiles to the growing force of Soviet counterforce missiles now being deployed in large numbers, and might opt for a dyad (two elements) system. Clearly Britain could not contemplate such a deterrent force.

The only valid argument for Britain maintaining a strategic nuclear force of any kind is that she should continue to contribute to the NATO nuclear force as the only European member able and willing to do so. France, of course, has a credible, independent nuclear deterrent based on the triad system, which she is maintaining and modernizing, but it is under strict national control and likely to remain so, unless and until France decides to rejoin the integrated military organization of NATO. Even then, it is not a foregone conclusion that a French government would assign its strategic nuclear force to NATO. It is a matter for speculation how long France can continue to maintain even her present nuclear deterrent in the face of rising costs and advances in technology, but she has already initiated plans for this decade and beyond. It is just possible that a new concept for an Anglo-French nuclear force might be proposed at some future date, despite the difficulties that frustrated similar plans in the early 'sixties and which still present problems. It is all the more important, therefore, that Britain should not abandon her nuclear force and her contribution to NATO, leaving France as the only European country with a strategic nuclear capability and one not assigned to NATO.

If, therefore, Britain decided to replace her existing force, and assuming that she is unable for economic reasons to produce and maintain more than one delivery system, she must decide on a system that will have a high degree of survivability and credibility, be capable of reaching important targets in the Soviet Union in the event of war, and have a life cycle lasting well into the next century. The factors that must be considered in arriving at a solution to Britain's problem are many and complex, and cannot be dealt with in detail here, but it is important to outline some of them and, in the process, to highlight the mistakes that have been made in the past, in the hope that similar errors of judgement will not be made again. If they are, they will be very expensive.

After the strikes at HMS *Neptune* (Faslane) in the summer of 1978, Britain must now accept that the kind of disruption by trade unions from which industry has suffered continuously under both Labour and Conservative Governments, and from which the Services have been relatively free, has now become a permanent threat to the successful operation of Polaris submarines. A handful of shop stewards could hold the entire force to ransom in pursuit of Communist inspired demands which a Labour Government would either have to meet or see the Polaris force confined to harbour. The policies of successive governments in 'civilianising' the dockyards, ports and other maintenance depots serving the Armed Forces, for the purpose of providing jobs and winning votes, irrespective of the damage which such policies might do to the operational efficiency of the Armed Forces, have provided the subversive elements in our society with a very powerful weapon. This is a new factor in deciding future defence policy which cannot be ignored, and the problems it presents could be expensive to solve.

The choices open to Britain in deciding which of the three launch environments, land, sea or air, to adopt, and the type of delivery vehicle by which warheads will be despatched to their targets, might well be heavily influenced by economic considerations rather than technical efficiency. It has been customary in recent years to assume that the submarine-launched ballistic missile system is the most survivable, the least vulnerable and the most suitable delivery system for Britain; yet it proved costly to acquire in 1962 even though the Americans agreed to a reduced price. But some of the factors which led to this judgement are either no longer applicable, or are about to be changed by new and greatly advanced technology. Submarines in dock or harbour are easy targets for Soviet fourth generation missiles such as the SS-18 and SS-19 or the SS-20 deployed specifically against European targets. They are also attractive objectives for the saboteur. When only four submarines are available, the credibility of such launch platforms is greatly reduced, because most of the time three will be in port. At sea, the launch platform enjoys a large measure of security from enemy attack when submerged on its action station, but it can be trailed and destroyed on its way to its launch area. The accuracy of a submarine-launched ballistic missile is, of course, likely to be less than that of a silo-based missile or a manned aircraft dropping free-fall bombs. If a single submarine is destroyed, or otherwise rendered inactive, all sixteen missiles are lost, and this applies whether the submarine is armed with ballistic or cruise missiles.

If, for economic or other reasons, Britain decided to continue with a sea-based strategic nuclear force, she could decide to build a new fleet of submarines (a minimum of five and preferably seven) with new missiles fitted with MIRV (Multiple Independently Targeted Re-entry Vehicle) warheads. She could either design and produce the missiles herself or buy them from the United States, as she did with Polaris. The choices would be between Poseidon and the Trident 1, both of which are MIRVed. If this proved to be economically unacceptable, Britain could modify the existing Polaris missiles (of which there is a plentiful supply in the United States) to take MIRV warheads, but a policy of buying off the shelf imposes dependence for logistic support on the United States, as is the case with Polaris today. Even if Britain continued to provide her own warheads, she would be dependent on the United States for constant use of the nuclear underground test facilities in the Nevada desert, so that she would virtually be totally subject to the United States for the efficient operation of her missiles and warheads.

Surface ships armed with cruise missiles must be ruled out for the same reasons that made them unacceptable fifteen years ago, when metaphorically the multilateral force (MLF) was politically and militarily torpedoed. Cruise missiles fired from submarines are a practicable proposition, but they will have to travel some distance over the sea before making a landfall on their way to their targets. It may prove easier to detect, plot and destroy them than similar missiles fired from land platforms or air-launched from manned aircraft. Ballistic missiles, irrespective of the type of platform from which they are launched may become vulnerable to new developments in anti-ballistic missile defences in the late 'eighties, especially from laser or charged particle beam weapons. Both the Soviet Union and, somewhat belatedly, the United States are devoting considerable efforts on research into these new and exotic systems of defence. The Soviets are ahead in charged particle beam development and will not be inhibited by any anti-ballistic missile (ABM) treaty that might be in force a decade from now.

Land-based ICBMs in hardened silos or on mobile launch platforms have a higher accuracy than submarine-launched systems, and would be used in a counterforce strike, whereas submarine-launched missiles are suitable for area or city targets. ICBMs are less restricted in throw-weight than submarine-launched missiles and their command and control system permits rapid response against hard targets in the event of pre-emptive attack by an enemy. But ICBMs in silos are becoming more vulnerable to first strike attack by the Soviet Union's fourth generation ICBMs, particularly the SS-18 and SS-19 with MIRV re-entry vehicles, which have a combination of yield and accuracy that would be sufficient to eliminate more than 80 per cent of United States Minuteman silos by the mid-'eighties. The United States must either further harden their Minuteman sites or introduce a new, mobile missile (MX), so as to present the Soviets with a more difficult first strike targeting problem. The only other course open to the United States would be to defend the silos with ABM defence systems which would breach the ABM treaty of 1972.

Britain could not possibly embark on a new and complicated system of ICBMs is silos or on mobile platforms, nor could she contemplate ABM defence systems. This leaves only the manned bomber concept, using ballistic missiles of the Skybolt type or cruise missiles. Free-fall or lay-down bombs could also be carried, but that would mean deep penetration of enemy defences, which even at low-level a decade from now would be a questionable proposition. The manned aircraft with cruise missiles is an attractive option, provided the superpowers do not limit the range and performance of the weapon to the extent that it would preclude Britain (or France) from adopting it for the strategic nuclear role. Such a combination would be cheaper than submarine-launched missiles and, because of the wide dispersal which can be adopted by manned aircraft, and the speed with which they can react to an attack by missiles, the launch platform would be much less vulnerable than submarines in dock or port. Britain has a great deal of experience with manned aircraft and stand-off missiles in both high and low-level modes and could produce both aircraft and missiles from national resources. She already has a good supply of nuclear warheads.

These are just some of the factors that Britain had to consider in deciding what system should replace the existing four Polaris submarines. It would be a sad reflection on Britain's status, even in Europe, if economic factors alone were to preclude replacement of the present strategic nuclear force. France has gone ahead with the development and modernization of her independent nuclear deterrent and will add a sixth submarine to her fleet in the early 1980s. She is also developing MIRV warheads for new missiles which will be fitted to the new submarine and possibly retrofitted to the existing fleet. With six submarines, it will be possible to maintain three on station all the time and sometimes four. If each missile carries four warheads independently targeted, then the strike capability of the submarine goes up from the present sixteen warheads on sixteen targets to sixty-four warheads on sixty-four targets. If all the existing submarines were to be fitted with the new MIRVed missiles (and assuming four on station), France would have the ability to deliver 256 warheads on 256 targets with the submarine force alone. It is possible that she will also fit MIRV warheads to her silo-based missiles (eighteen), adding a further seventy-two warheads, and by maintaining her Mirage bomber force (thirty-three) France could produce a grand total of 361 warheads in a triad system of six submarines, eighteen silo-based missiles and thirty-three Mirage bombers. The problem of increasing vulnerability of silo-based systems applies equally to France and the United States, but more particularly to France, now that the Soviets have deployed the SS-20 MIRVed missile targeted on Europe.

Being outside the NATO integrated military organization, France quietly ignores accusations that by increasing and improving her strategic nuclear force she is being provocative to the Soviet Union. France showed her determination to become an independent nuclear power under de Gaulle in 1962 and to remain a nuclear power. She has not deviated from that objective despite difficulties and set-backs in creating her nuclear force which Britain was spared by her close ties with the United States.

In a television interview on 16th October 1978, just three weeks after the announcement that France was to add a sixth submarine to her existing strategic nuclear fleet, President Giscard d'Estaing proudly stated, without fear of contradiction, that France was the world's third nuclear power, ahead of Britain. She had the third highest standard of living and was the fifth greatest economic power. France, the President said, had overtaken Britain as far back as 1967 in terms of gross national product and if she continued to observe the directions for steady economic growth which the government and private industry urged the population to follow, France could become an economic power on a par with West Germany in less than a decade. One might well ask where this leaves strike-ridden Britain, dominated by left-wing politicians and trade unions who, lemming-like, appear to be determined to destroy themselves and the economy of the country, having first disarmed it.

Britain and France will feel the effects of rising costs and advancing technology in this decade, whatever systems they decide to operate in their efforts to maintain some form of strategic nuclear capability. The time may come when France will decide that her present strategy is unrealistic (many senior officers in the Armed Forces are already condemning the present defence policy) and that her interests would be better served by rejoining the integrated command structure of NATO. If that should happen, then the prospects for a collaborative agreement between Britain and France to produce a satisfactory contribution to NATO's strategic nuclear forces would be much brighter and the cost would be considerably less than each country will have to pay for separate development.

Britain has decided to acquire the United States Trident submarine ballistic missile system at a cost currently estimated at £5000 million for deployment in the 1990s. But in a decade from now the cost will have escalated to more like £7000 million and in the intervening years, while the new system is being produced, other more important conventional weapons systems will have to be cancelled to meet the enormous cost of the Trident system. From a strategic and cost-effective point of view Trident is the wrong system for Britain and the Government may live to regret the decision. The cruise missile would have been a more effective, more credible and a much cheaper system.

Index

Index